I'M NOT
CHINESE

I'M NOT
CHINESE

A Tale of Satori, Cooking and Self-Discovery

OBRY ALAN

AuthorReputationPress®
Creativity & Branding

Author Reputation Press LLC
45 Dan Road Suite 36
Canton MA 02021
www.authorreputationpress.com
Hotline: 1(800) 220-7660
Fax: 1(855) 752-6001

Ordering Information:
Quantity sales. Special discounts are available on quantity purchases by corporations, associations, and others. For details, contact the publisher at the address above.

Printed in the United States of America.

ISBN-13:   Softcover   978-1-951343-33-0
           eBook   978-1-951343-34-7

Library of Congress Control Number: 2019913826

Dedicated to Glenda, with me through all that
madness and everything good I know about love.

Obry Alan

Dec. 2, 2018

CONTENTS

wonderful things are waiting to happen, and should expect them. Cooking up deals, brainstorming no cost-low cost advertising and making numbers 'tumble'. Star ship Noodle launching into the market place. Financials; the life-blood of business and learning to avoid anemia. Everything that sells something's got to be good. Doing what's needed getting done being Chinese, by not being Chinese at all.

A carnival based perspective for market analysis elucidated by a venerated vending elder and reluctant perfect master. This marketing wisdom centers on 'learning lessons #2 and #3, for sure, which is to know what you don't know you don't know, for sure...' Also, learning to learn about what you need to do, and how to make the choices you make in life that'll bring you closer to your own long- term happiness as taught by a human Yoda.

Glenda finally arrives, an afternoon repose. Learning the greatest of all lessons in life: that money is the one thing nobody wants to talk about. Learning to make numbers tumble. Learning rule # 3, products that sell themselves. What clients expect from the temple of possibilities, and selling chances to experience dreams.

Learning Rule # 4: You talking to me...? Making use of things never being what they seem. Entering the temple of possibilities, taking chances, experiencing dreams. How things work in parallel universes. Never playing games that can't be won. Rule # 5: No one ever talks about juice. Business being what everything is all about.

When things go wrong and you can't send in the clowns or call in Ghost busters, who you gonna call? Can you believe that angels really show up to save the day? Believe it. Discovering that what happens in life; is about a power much greater than yourself so believe it when it happens.

Someone watching over wanting to have fun; what could possibly go wrong? Things to think about when contemplating jumping off the world. Learning most things are out of your control and accepting that, and to go on from there. Realizing my mind's a beautiful thing to waste and the need to 'get away' to think about it.

Wisdom comes with doing, and has its own cost. Defining the word enough. Poisoning our minds with good intentions and going full circle being my own worst enemy. Success becoming my own undoing. No need for Munchkins. When you need to start screaming. Watching the best movie of my life. Going on, from there into everything that's good.

A strange little man explains the meaning of life and living.

No need for Munchkins when you need to start screaming. Watching the best movie of my life. Going on, from there into everything that's good.

Tasting colors. When too much, is more than just enough. Knowing ingredients. Woking and rolling as fast as you can. Getting started. Tools of the trade. What goes on before anything gets cooked. Techniques for preparing and wok cooking Asian recipes. Ingredients explained.

APPENDIX

Movies help to shape our lives and our ideas, after all, if you are what you eat, you are also what you think, and what you think is shaped by what you see and what you believe.

CHAPTER 1

'IN THE BEGINNING IS ALWAYS CONFUSION'

'LIFE AS A WORK IN PROGRESS'

Doesn't everyone dream of or; dare imagining working for themselves? Running their own shows and taking charge of their own lives while living the dream of making the big bucks entrepreneurs claim as their own? Of positioning yourself, in the lucrative income streams of anything that requires working at all to be worthwhile? I have. That's what this story's about. And in this thirty-year process of self-discovey, trying to live the dream of my life, sold over sixteen tons of noodles, fourteen tons of rice and thousands and thousands of egg rolls trying to discover who I was. Or; in this case, who I wasn't, hence the title, because, I really am not Chinese. And it wasn't easy not being Chinese yet, ended up being one of the best parts of my life as I busied myself getting it all got done. And then that, dragged on as a reasonably successful business for thirty years. Keep in mind; that nothing ever gets done, or ever has, until it gets done, until progress of some kind has been made at getting something accomplished, whatever that 'it', may be. When you begin seeing yourself living your life from this perspective, it becomes obvious right away, that you, are your own work in progress, implying that whether or not you realize it, you're experiencing the inexorable effects of living your dreams. Of inter-acting with the world around you and; getting results. How you work with the results you get is what you, taking charge of your life and being you, is all about. This, is how I became not Chinese, from the beginning, it was me, experiencing the very 'unbearable lightness of being' that living can be when you decide to search for your own happiness. Inter-acting with the world around you is what fuels your experiences, and what fuels your experiences, is you, imagining living the dream of your life. Crazy huh? It's not so much a question of whether or not your cup's either half full or half empty so much as it's about, where do you go from there, living your life as a dream coming true. This is especially true if you're at all ambitious. Or motivated by believing and searching for that indescribable something you haven't yet experienced. Perhaps even benefiting from having something that's yours, and yours' alone, something you've created or built, something that drives you to keep looking forward, thinking about tomorrow, because success is more likely to be found by looking forward rather than backward. Therefore, it's pretty obvious that taking charge of the circumstances of your life becomes, the most essential element of progress in living it. I'd subscribe to that, maybe even urge you to consider considering it, because; if you don't know what's going on in your life, or feel like events and circumstances are out of control, relax, you're not alone. But before beginning at the beginning and starting to imagine your future, it becomes necessary for you to make peace with yourself about your past. Truth is; not knowing or reconciling yourself to your past makes it that much more likely you'll be repeating it again until you get yourself right. Though practice may make perfect, repeating things and not learning from your experiences, is not always a desirable option for living a satisfying life. And I'd agree; that life itself can sometimes get in the way of just living it, which increases the difficulty of having to learn some things twice. So, getting to know yourself first, suggests that your past is the key to imagining your future, to unlocking your potential, and begin living your dreams. I mean, what're you waiting for? You don't need to be some visionary or anything, you just put that key in that lock, set yourself free, and never look back or regret anything that helps you become who ever your are or want to be. Actually, even just thinking about that, springing that lock and setting yourself free by considering your dreams, is what progress is all about.

Considerations like these make clear the underlying need to stop doing things the same old way and trying to satisfy yourself with getting the same old results, and forcing yourself to believe you're happy with that, all the while believing there's something more. Recognizing instead, maybe even for the first time, the benefits of doing things in new ways, reveals everything the past is likely to bring back to you in the future, your future.

For example, after a while of living my dreams, I really needed to get away, not so much to think about the past, but for considering the future. I was looking forward to it, and had been for a long time.

The strangest thing about finally getting away from the last twenty-five years however, was the harder I tried not thinking about it, the more I thought of nothing else. I mean really, who in their right mind finally gets away from everything making them crazy, only to spend all their time thinking about what they were bothering to try getting away from, instead of looking forward to relaxing and enjoying themselves? About the only thing I was certain of at all; was that I hadn't wanted to get away, only to keep thinking about the same thing over and over every time I closed my eyes trying to relax. There was no denying the need to get away though, for taking time off to think about the future, for wanting to get some really needed perspective on life, my life. Which had begun feeling like an endless sit-com; strangers in the supermarket began asking me, if I was that 'Chinese' guy and I couldn't respond because I wasn't any longer even sure myself. Other shoppers overhearing this gave me really weird looks. This is what success brings I remember thinking; believing I needed to escape from my own life. And to do that, while avoiding, as completely as possible, thinking about the 'great idea' that was supposed to bring me joy and fulfillment. You know, success, freeing me up, setting me up for living the good life in my older years. Well, that was then, which was a long time ago, and now, now was now, more than twenty-five years later, with lots of water having gone over the dam so to speak, and I wasn't feeling freed up as much as feeling trapped. I reasoned I wouldn't keep thinking the same things, over and over again like my brain was broken, if things were great. But they weren't, and I knew I'd gone almost full circle, knew also, that found at the end of every circle is truth, that's basic geometry. Work smarter, my inner voice kept telling me, when you're young, so you won't have to work that hard when you're older. Playing that same message over and over again like a loop tape in my psyche, isn't that pretty much the mantra? Made me sometimes wish my brain had a volume control, or a pause button or something. Well, time had passed and I wasn't young any longer, or feeling excessively peaceful about that either. And, to complicate that, every time I went on vacation and tried relaxing by a mountain stream or something, trying to forget, or remember, or meditate, stretched out there on some rocks in a sunbeam, eyes closed, trying to see the future, only a second or two would go by before finding myself remembering things I meant to never forget and forgetting things I'd promised myself I'd always remember. I couldn't stop thinking about how time had passed and I'd ended up here, with plenty of mixed feelings about success, all these years later. Hey, running a business of your own is exciting, it's wonderful, the cash is great, the events exciting; the people; I'll never forget them, but remember, it's work, just like any other job, only you're responsible for a whole lot more. I'd built a successful small business from nothing more than just an idea, but then, as time went by, felt something just wasn't any longer right and denying it to myself made me feel like I was losing my mind.

Especially when I tried relaxing and forgetting about all the stuff that stressed me out, employees, deliveries, schedules, you name it. After all; who can ever know, or guess, where living the days of your life will lead, which is probably a better arrangement for us and most importantly, without us even knowing about it. Still, try imagining trying to find happiness in your life living with knowable expiration dates? But even the best plans and intentions are easily derailed by fate and circumstances, which can leave you sometimes at best, just following along, doing whatever you can to keep it all together. So now, there I was, those days having led to a place for considering everything that'd occurred so far in my life. Fate having me find myself where I did, helpless to resisting the endless wondering about success and failure every time I closed my eyes trying to see my way forward into the future. Looking back seemed no way for seeing my way into the future. Never, would I've guessed things could've played out as they had, that I'd be left feeling so unsure about everything. Success, I had always assured myself, was supposed to bring you up, to the next level of self-realization, self- actualization. The entire episode of my 'career' left me feeling a very unlikely business success story. On the other hand, had I not been even moderately successful, I probably wouldn't've remained in business for all those years, especially at the expense of making myself crazy. Secretly, I loved that which made me craziest, and because of that believed I'd earned my success, but now, looking back, trying to relax, realized I'd learned it, and earned it, and a lot of other lessons, the hard way.

Inheriting had never been an option, or family help of any kind, or anticipating anything for making life easier, you know, like a distant rich Uncle Freddie to count on when he…you know, no longer needed it. But once I began putting my mind to it, using my ideas like a map or a reciepe, things began getting done and got done, by me, doing things my way, which believe it or not, wasn't always that bad. Truth is, I was making it up and faking it as I went along doing and saying whatever I needed to, to make things happen, all aimed at being successful. Things sometimes even just working out inspired me, making me hungry for more, and sometimes, even working out better than even I ever expected them to. Some things though, like taking charge of my life and working for myself, just made more sense, compared to thinking about getting a job, any job I might get, or all the rest of that static. Maybe I got lucky and made a bunch of right guesses, because success depends heavily on a good amount of guesswork, and more often than not, freaky good luck, but always, lots of motivated personality. And really, I'm not that lucky, I don't waste money I don't have, buying lottery tickets or gambling, hoping to get 'lucky'. Working for yourself is enough of a gamble. So, I've tried contenting myself with being happy, living my own best dream.

If anything, I've worked hard at making those dreams come true. I'm not saying I'm unlucky; stranger things than luck have happen in my life. What I'm saying is I've worked hard attempting to become successful at something I dreamed up and imagined as possible. Along the way, some things just seemed more obvious to me as better choices almost for certain, as if I'd intuited them, because, I've always had a 'feeling' about what might, or might not, be the right thing at the right time.

Especially a thing that's the right thing at the right time and in business, that's about taking advantage of opportunity. So, I'll tell you this: Trying to find yourself too late in life, after not believing enough in yourself for most of it, almost always sets you up for disappointment. Particularly forever wanting to know in the first place, but mostly, for waiting too long to get your life under way. You might be living like life was a forever thing until you come to know that it isn't, and from that moment on everything that happens onward into your future, is everything about who you've been, who you are and all the possibilities about who you might yet become or what you still might accomplish. It might be as simple as simply changing your mind about how you've been living your life and the choices you've already made. Because changing your mind and changing your thinking is the one thing you can always do to begin doing something to help yourself. Trust me on this, and this, is what I've learned, there's always a time for checking things out, and the sooner you figure out when those times are, the better off you're going to be. End; of sermon. Most times, in my experience, you've got to learn trusting in your own common sense, especially when no one around you is going to tell you, or even let on about anything that might jeprodise their own good fortune. 'You'll figure it out...' they always say, as if that lets them off the hook for being helpful at all.

Truth is, most people feel helping someone out, unfairly disadvantages them; for doing a good deed. But, when it comes to doing business... that's the way a lot of people begin thinking.

Listen, I'm no Einstien but after I started trying to operate a Szechuan take out concession profitably, even I figured out early in my concessionairing career that the time for checking things out at events wasn't when things were going full bang ahead. No, I'm not that kind of curious anyway; to me, work is work, either you're at work or you're not. And when I was at work, I was hard at work and my only interest primarily, was that the crowds of people at those shows we were doing, were the groups I'd identified as 'my people'. You try selling anything in the wrong market to people who don't take you or your product seriously, you're finished, so don't expect too much. Or, be prepared to work that much harder to compete with other business forces. Maybe that sounds a bit cynical, but that's just the way things are, harsh maybe, but true.

What I am, is a guy that doesn't like loosing after playing any game, as hard as a guy needs to play games that are that hard to play. And it was a game. A game I decided to get really good at playing. Really good at, as good as I could possibly get, but let me tell you, trying to be that good, at anything, is eventually bound, to piss somebody off, maybe even become the worst thing you could do for yourself working that hard to be successful. Imagine that?

Right away it became obvious that when you play someone else's games, the rules can be changed at any time, and you lose. No matter what, that's what happens when you're playing someone else's games. But when you play your own games, you can make the rules up, if you have to, as you go along, sometimes, even changing them when you need to, and if that doesn't sound like good incentive for being in business for yourself, you're probably late for work.

Besides, by the time any of these events I'm going to be telling you about, started really gathering momentum, say, along with the second or third band, with any luck, we'd be deep into crazy, and that's the way it went, usually, until the show was over. That was the way I liked it best. That, I discovered early on, was the way money was made, not by walking around looking to see what was going on with everybody else. At those times, things were just so busy, it didn't seem like work at all, and so focused was I on what we were doing, nothing else mattered. Except maybe, what time it was. I was well aware that the portal of profitability was only open for so long, and that's kind of why it was like being on an episode of Star Trek. We had to pass through that portal of profitability before the show ended and it closed back up, just like a black hole. So I guess I owe part of my success not only to Rock and Roll, but a deep understanding of science and Star Trek, too.

I don't even recall the music the shows were all about either, even as it was being played, even though musical events were our specialty. I just wasn't there to listen; it was just massive background noise, even though music is a very important part of my life, just not as much so when I'm at work. But musical-events were what we were all about. Especially two or three day shows with lots of repeat customers, customers who were an actual captive audience of hungry of partiers with money to spend on having a good time. Groups of folks, all kinds of folks, families all in tie dyed outfits, lots of them with kids, glad to see us back again, vending for another year. Friendships with people like these, at shows like these evolved over a number of years where we'd only see them once or twice a year for a day or two, but for the last twelve or fifteen years or longer. So, in total, our friendships were like less than a month old but were the basis of wonderful, enduring friendships. A lot of these folks were, older, straight type people you'd never suspect finding at a music festival, teachers, dentists, lawyers, hedge fund type professionals, all bare foot, wearing tie-dyed T- shirts, partying and just generally giving it up like they were still young. Cool, but pretty weird. God bless them, but they were my target audience. They afforded what is known as unrestrained discretionary spending.

I've often wondered if I'd be concerned if I knew my dentist was stoned as he yanked out a tooth? I guess I'm OK with that, as long as he is, and providing, I suppose, that he gets the right tooth. These people, were there to 'let go' and let their inner child run amok for two or three days without adult supervision, I was there to make sure they ate properly while they raved on.

The average profile of these partiers, who were our market share, was that they were good kids. But there were always the numerous space cadets you'd expect to find, who'd lost their coolers, however you go about losing a cooler. Or had forgotten their backpacks. Or; had forgotten they were still wearing them.

Or had left them in the cars they'd hitched rides in, but were very willing, as they always explained, to barter for food. And that; is very coded language if ever there was, and at rock concerts you can probably imagine what they were talking about bartering with. And so, while all this public relations kind of stuff, was taking place, we cooked as hard and as fast and for as long as we could. I tell you it was insane because the music was usually so loud; it was like a work place hazard, like working in an insane asylum, where you literally; couldn't even hear yourself think. And we haven't even begun talking about working crowds where some of the partiers had grossly over- drugged their grade levels and were standing there staring bewildered, ordering food from the shores of some distant star system, blinking and staring, with looks of incredible wonder and blank confusion on their faces. Working these shows became like dosing on reality T.V., only better, more real, about as real as it can ever get. I began thinking of my job as spontaenous, interactive improv theatre that went on sometimes for sixteen hours a day and long into the night.

Man, sometimes it took days after these shows to recover mentally and physically, our ears would still be ringing, even after using earplugs. You'd think these bands playing were making an effort to be clearly heard in Europe. But being as close to the stage as I could get, was where I'd learned the action really is, always is, and so, there, it was, we were, so to speak. But most importantly, I wasn't there to dance or party or listen to the music, I was there to sell as many pounds of noodles as I could and doing all three of those things at the same time was just to over the top for even me to think about it. I was there to sell as much Chinese food as I possibly could in a limited time span vending egg-rolls, chicken fingers, cold noodles vegetable rice, shrimp, and the weight of a Buick in noodles weighing on me. I was heavily invested not only financially, but in my own wellbeing and profitable future as well and, as always, there was a big nut to crack before I ever made even a dime for all my effort.

The general operating proceedure was to pay to play and I was paying to play hard as I could, for as long as it took to get rid of all the noodles and everything else I'd shown up with and was intensely motivated financially by everything necessary to operate as a business, being required 'up front'. Even after we got popular as the place to eat at events, it still took a while to unload several hundred pounds of noodles, per day, one order at a time. But, we did it, did it over and over again for so many times, we lost track and began just estimating the poundage of noodles each show required by the year before. This required large coolers on wheels so full of noodles they were almost impossible to lift. So you can trust me when I tell you that it took some time to get rid of them all. At that point though, once the show began, time was on our side. We had a captive audience. And here, I'm talking about doing twelve, fourteen, even sixteen-hour days, two or three days in a row, endlessly cooking. Staying at my station, doing what I'd come there to do, like Kirk on the bridge of the Enterprise, in complete control, calling for more eggrolls, more noodles, more of everything.

When the clock on the wall eventually broke, (the minute hand stopped going around and it remained always one-thirty), I never bothered fixing it, because it just stopped mattering. We were there for the duration.

We were always the very first people on the lot to show up, get set up and be heavily into selling before other vendors had pulled their acts together, and then, the last to leave when things were over, selling everything right up to the end when there was no else there but us. At that point, the inside of the trailer looked like complete food chaos. Seeing other vendors walking around after a show began, told me everything I needed to know about their business, that them walking around was likely to see what kind of business we were doing that they weren't.

As a vendor, especially after paying huge fees and expenses and having a very limited windows of opportunity, walking around after a show began was for amateurs and beginners and generally, people who just didn't know what they were doing or how to go about getting it done. We on the other hand, knew our routine. We were there to make income incoming as fast as possible, and usually, once events began, they rapidly began taking on a life of their own very quickly. Our mission, (my business plan), was to secure at least ten percent of the total wave, work it as hard as we could, and then ride that wave all the way into the beach. Ten percent wasn't impossible, twenty percent was where insanity began, especially whether you wanted it or not. It was like a human wave washing over you tsunami like, and when you surfaced, dazed, people were shouting at you about more eggrolls or noodles, and waving money at you, and what began as a dream coming true, began seeming more like a food nightmare that didn't seem to have an end, and freaking out simply wasn't an option. So, showing up early to work was the time for experiencing the calm before the storm. Crowds seemed to get really weird when they we're hungry all at the same time. Usually, these events would be a ghost town and the only other people there'd be bands doing final sound checks that echoed loudly in otherwise completely empty festival arenas, tuning up for the show I'd never hear once the event began and got under way.

The preternaturally quiet mornings would begin becoming more alive as crowds queuing up at the entrance gates provided a palpable nervous, excited energy, like cattle getting ready to stampede. Energy that'd be overwhelmingly released once the gates were open and they flooded in as the show began. At that point, experience taught, there'd be no turning back, no denying the game definitely being on, and remaining on, at full blast, until the very last act of the day, later that night, when those same crowds began leaving after a long exhausting day of giving it up and dancing, partying and having fun. Slowly shuffling aimlessly along like a bunch of played out fun zombies, languidly drifting sullenly along in a dream like state, lugging the same chairs, umbrellas, and now, empty coolers they'd come with, as if they'd been on an all day, twenty-mile forced fun hike. It can actually be quite exhausting having that much of a good time.

But in the mornings, before anything at all began, the only requirement for me, was one quick, final inspection that the machine's main spring had been adequately wound to the point of hair trigger release. That meant that everything was in place for facilitating the unknown volumes of fun about to be had, prior to blast off. Before the crowds surged in with their determined hedonistic abandon, more than adequately encumbered, laden with coolers, folding chairs and sun umbrellas. As usual, I'd tie on my apron, cinching it professionally, taking one last meaningful samurai-like look at the broken clock on the wall, not being surprised to see it still at one-thirty, as if it really mattered at all, realizing it was going to be another long days journey into night before this day was over.

But now, things were different and had really changed since we'd started doing 'the stand'. Now; it seemed events were only just beginning and already there'd be a jostling, snaking line of people in front of the concession trailer, waiting lines of hungry people, going back as far as I could see without my glasses, craning their necks sideways from behind the people in front of them, trying to determine if the line, my line, was moving at all.

It made me wonder who ate Chinese food that early except maybe Chinese people, not even considering it as my good fortune. I was such a beginner then, I can only laugh at myself in retrospect.

But I knew what was happening was happening because I was the one who had caused it to happen. It was I, after all, who had intentionally caused the captivating, wafting aromas of garlic and ginger sizzling in roasted sesame oil and rice wine vinegar to hypnotically summon their patronage. They, for their part, were there to have fun and spend money. I knew that; and knew also, that I was there to entice them to spend it at our joint. And so that; became my primary mission and sole objective. Actually, I had determined that they would spend it at our concession if I had any opportunity to influence their decision-making. And I did, so I did, and I did everything I could think of doing to do just that.

In a personal, secretive way, I felt kind of like the pied piper. Well aware of the effects of the tune I played. And our clients, for their part as mice, or hamsters, or clients or what ever, simply, irresistibly, willingly, followed their noses, then, opened their wallets. This hadn't just occurred by luck though, or, by random mere happenstance. I'd meant for it to happen just the way I had imagined it happening, and had planned on having it happen, but was still plenty surprised when it actually did.

It made me feel I was on to something big, something new and exciting, something, adventurous and exceptionally renumerative.

Early on, while making my bones in the 'carney school of economics', working all the grade 'b' shows that'd have me, I learned everything, from the basics of slight of hand to double and even triple entry accounting procedures, and got an education that turned out to be better than doing advanced work at Harvard. Most importantly, it was about learning about peope. I learned that sometimes in life, as in business, 'you've just got to do, what you've got to do', the rest of it, you make up as you go along, hoping for the best. And so, when things really began happening, I began understanding the power of getting what you hoped for, making it happen by knowing your buying audience and identifying and thinking of them as, my people. At this point in my vending career I enthusiastically employed every trick in the unwritten vendor's code of ethical (and reasonably ethical) behavior handbook that I could think of to bolster business. I was honing my sales craft amongst the old timers I found myself concessing amongst in all the grade 'b' shows who politely thought of someone who wasn't Chinese selling Chinese food as either completely wacky, or maybe a genius but untested business angle that had potential, and it was them who began refering to us as 'the Chinese people'.

'Where's that smell coming from' was the most common question people'd ask the vending elders, only to be told, 'from the 'Chinese people' who weren't even Chinese at all they'd say, so go figure.

But it was because of them, all the old 'Carnies' we 'played' with, that we managed to invent a few new angles on the game for ourselves. I was remember after all, involved in learning to play a game, my game, refining its rules, rules with possibilities I was learning to know better than anyone else, and so why bother even playing a game at all, unless you intend to win? When those shows were over; that was it, people scattered as it got dark and abandoned the scene and if you hadn't made back your seed investment by then, and hopefully, some on top of that for all your hard work, well too bad for you and, hard cheese old boy, better luck next time. Things began revealing themselves to me and those old timers nickle and diming away their week ends weren't about to impart anything to me that'd make me more competitive with them than I needed to be, especially and particularly by not even being Chinese. Amongst themselves, they thought I was out of my mind not realizing I was pioneering my way into selling healthy vegetarian food at traditionally 'fried-fried' carnival food venues, because at that time, nobody was doing it. I could have the field to myself if I wanted it, and I did, even if it meant doing it and not being Chinese at the same time.

In the vending world, like I mentioned earlier, windows of opportunity are limited by the beginning and endings of a show, so, if why you're there doesn't happen between those two points, it's probably not going to happen at all, so, sorry, better luck next time. In addition to that, remember, that by the beginning of an event, a sizable financial commitment had to be recouped before even hitting a break-even point; only after that gamble would it be pay-off time for all that hard work. And for the gamble that it was, and all the hard work that that gamble required, I learned early, that the fruits of ones own labor are always sweeter, just harder to get at. Remember, if doing pretty much anything in life was easier, you can be sure more people would be trying to do it. Just don't ever forget that things that look easy usually aren't, and the people doing them, making them look that easy, have usually done those things many times before.

Trust me, it's less about how simple something looks, and more about what you're not seeing that's important. Losing, or coming up short wasn't an option though, and so once the game was on, I was seriously committed and motivated to play as hard, and, for as long as it took to ensure a profitable day. And I played hard too, often until way late at night, and it's important that you should know that I couldn't do it by myself. I had help, and I paid that help very well to motivate them into playing that hard and that long along with me. It was wholesome, chaotic fun, with live music in the background. How many jobs or careers can offer that? I became an employer, and by paying my help a good wage, enabled them to help themselves have a better life. Quickly, I came to see, just how money was made, especially in such limited windows of opportunity. It was all about being prepared, about how you made numbers tumble into profit, but more on that later. Believe me, you never make any money saying 'one dollar' over and over all day long. You'd just work yourself out for short return and still be at work at that rate. It became important about presenting the message before ever presenting the product. That was what I had to figure out, how to let people know I was there when they didn't. It involved theatre and a confident 'on stage' presence.

The first few orders of every show were fun, done primarily as advertising for the benefit of the larger crowd who hadn't yet made up their minds about what to eat, or where. What better advertising in a crowd is there, than seeing someone walk by devouring a beautiful, fragrant, delicious looking platter loaded with Chinese food? An advertising medley of colorful vegetables and piles of house special chicken or shrimp on a sauce glistening mountain of oriental noodles? Walking and eating, saying 'yum' between mouthfuls, people, I noticed, notice things like this. I made a mental note and turned my clients into my advertising technique, which was much better than any stationary sign that had to be read could ever solicit. And… there's virtually no advertising as effective as the unsolicited testimonial. Our product began speaking for itself. It became a product that sold itself. It was a product that if you were hungry at all, would tell you you needed this, because only this would make the day complete. Imagine my sense of good fortune.

Suddenly, the tempo of events would begin inching up, getting louder and faster, crowds more boisterous, the beat driving me to cook faster and faster, in three woks, all at the same time, all on high flame. I could feel by this point in the show, whether or not it was going to be a good day, and when you feel confident about things like that, not even swimming the English channel seems too daunting. I began stiring and saucing to the tempo like an automaton, thinking, I can do this.

But like I say; watch out, things aren't always as they appear. This was the perfect recipe for potential disaster by anyone less than a master; (known in China as Daai See Fooh, or, Grand Maestro of the Culinary Arts), disaster brought on by a simple, single moment of inattention, or excess hubris. Flames shooting high and woks loudly sizzling was like working on the high wire, surrounded by watching people, working without the security benefit of a net below. One slip, one fall, one simple misplaced ladel movement mixing brocolli with shrimps could spell disaster. Nervously, my mind floated as I cooked concerned that I'd finally gotten what I'd prayed for, realizing all I could do was keep my head down, stay focused and keep cooking as fast as I could, without worrying about going insane and realizing I'd never realize it even if I did. So I did just that. This wasn't a movie in my mind, this was real life, with, a killer soundtrack, not some dress rehearsal with food, and I grew to love every wild, frenzied moment of it. And believe me, it often got frenzied, but I felt more alive then, going crazy, than I ever remembered feeling, and as happy too.

Within an hour or so of the show opening, I'd be in the 'zone' along with the usual cast of characters, focused entirely on what we were doing, afraid to look up at the lengthening line of hungry partiers. I was actually being happy; I was giddy, it could have been for the first time in my entire life. We were shifting into higher gear. The music clearly getting even louder, and faster, but mostly louder, like someone operating the soundboard had just found the volume control, dramatically amping it up.

Food began flying. Szechuan peppers sizzling their pungent, aromatic smoke making everyone's' 'eyes tear up, choking clients around the counters. The bands' loudness, hiding the sounds of ingredients violently hissing as they cooked, making hearing new orders almost impossible. The muted, explosive bubbly roar of egg rolls and chicken fingers plunging into the deep fryer made everything else harder to hear. We fell into operating as if on autopilot, knowing our jobs, and working madly at them like a team of highly coordinated oriental food robots.

I stole another quick, meaningless glance at the clock on the wall, still one-thirty, as usual, but knew it wasn't even lunchtime yet, and it was going to be like this until closing time at eleven o'clock that night.

That realization made me panicky, afraid of freaking out under the pressure, and the only reason I didn't, was realizing I was getting what I'd wished for. Don't ever; even for a moment, think success is easy, or, pretty. But more importantly, be careful of what you wish for, because you just might get it. Wishing though, is wishing, success is doing. Success is just you, doing what you've got to do to keep from freaking out just to get through, what you know you've got to do. And it can get pretty sketchy at times.

Between acts at these three-day musical festivals, the M.C. of the show often felt compelled, I guessed, to announce from the stage that there were also other vendors to make purchases from without saying 'besides the Chinese people'. That was us.

But the line of people in front of our concession seemed to keep growing longer not any shorter, without a single person defecting to another vendor. Lucky us, huh? I wondered if I should be somehow embarrassed, but we weren't forcing anyone to give us their business. I simply figured we had what they wanted, isn't that what business is supposed to be about any way?

I was terrified to look up, I knew they were all standing there watching, and waiting, so I concentrated on doing what I'd come there to do, a thing I did best, and cooked Chinese food like a wild man. I was on stage and there was a lot of entertaining theatre about watching me cook without any attendant disasters. It was my version of food choreography, ballet of the noodle conducted by the wave of my cooking spatual baton. All those woks going, was like working at the equator. It was easily about one hundred degrees there in front of the deep fryer, with all the woks blazing away and our giant rice cooker steaming and bubbling on these gorgeous summer days. Cooking that insanely made me feel like a contestant on the Asian cooking game show version of 'beat the clock'. How many orders could I put out in five minutes?

Two minutes? Approaching what we called the 'lunch crowd' I realized I hadn't stopped or left my duty station since we began that morning, and the line seemed to continue getting even longer. But now, with lunchtime approaching, even longer. I'd trained myself for situations like these not to panic, but to slow down and work at my own pace. If they were going to leave, they'd leave, but they never did. After all, there was really only so fast I could cook.

All good things take time, even Benjamin Franklin knew that haste made waste, but I don't think he was talking just about cooking Chinese food. He could've been, but it's unlikely. So, I cooked, and as I did, I mused about why be concerned? I'd grown this business since it's humble beginnings, when people told me all the time that 'I didn't look Chinese'. My only response in those days was saying; 'only on the outside'. That left them with faces twisted up with looks of perplexed confusion. And I liked that, it was kind of like silent pay back. Now, hardly anybody ever said 'flied lice, 'chop- chop' or shouted several times, 'numabh fooh' or anything unintentionally derogatory or unfunny like that any more. Now, they just watched, paid, and ate and usually tipped. Just a couple minutes of watching our operation spoke volumes about making Chinese food, and that, was all about making serious Chinese bread. And that kind of dough was nothing to laugh at. But it took time to get good enough at doing it and growing to this point, before; amongst the other vendors, we became a force to be reckoned with. Mostly it came with getting better and, being better prepared. In a business like this, it teaches that it's always better to have more than you need and not need it than to need it and not have it, and that goes for almost everything in life. So I learned to wind the machine by being as prepared as a Szechuan vending business on the road could possibly be.

I'd come to think of preparing for an event as, 'arming the stand' and 'winding the machine' because once a show began and got under way, our stand operated like a machine spring, un-springing. We tried to profitably control that un-winding and did a lot better than I ever imagined we would've. What I unfortunately was learning at the time though, without even knowing it, is that sometimes your success can be the exact reason for your demise. That being too good, as I mentioned earlier, can bring on the giant kiss off. But things like that take time to learn and become manifest and I hadn't yet gotten that far in my career of not being Chinese, but eventually would. But believe me, at times of all out vending chaos such as these music festivals, the machine unwinding like a giant main spring wildly, maniacally uncoiling at an explosive rate taking on a life of its' own. You hold on and do your best but things at any moment can easily spiral out of control. By the end of the day, there'd be food detritus everywhere in the trailer. Eggrolls that had been stepped on three or four times, burnt noodles dangling, brocolli florettes as flat as postage stamps on the floor, and everything at the end of the show had to be cleaned before opening again the next day, usually in less than six hours. Those early days of vending now seem nostalgically peaceful, like they'd occurred hundreds of years ago, or at least many tons of noodles ago. No joke, tons of noodles ago.

Then, suddenly, my dream bubble revelry would pop, and I'd tune back into the show like a panic attack, feeling like a machine stuck in the on position doing the same thing over and over without even thinking about it. It reminded me of all of the people who'd asked me over the years, how I ever learned to cook Chinese food. And I always told them the same thing; that I was still learning, and that was the truth, and when you do anything over and over literally thousands of times, you either get better at it or have a mental breakdown. Maybe that, I feared, was what I had to look forward to. But then, wasn't the time to worry about it.

No, now, there was no stopping, no turning back, quitting wasn't even a remote option, and I felt quite certain, quitting at that point would've started a riot. Trust me on this; I know how emotional hungry people can get. Especially if they've been patiently standing, waiting in a line that doesn't seem to be moving. There'd be no Christian understanding if I freaked, and I knew it. There'd be no; 'what'y mean the guy had a mental break down? So what? That's too bad, I'm hungry where's my order?' Hungry people can be as emotionally taciturn as wild animals. I knew this to be the number one rule in business; fortunately for me I had protection, I would've been crazy not to have. I had a firewall in place that'd never fail me. I think. Listen, I never could've carried this madness off alone, I tried that years before and learned the hard way about the importance of good help. And now, I had great help. The quality and caliber of my help was fundamental to my business success. That's why I always paid them so good; I depended upon them, and needed them to help me be successful, and they too needed me to be successful so I could keep on paying them. And that; is not the sound of one hand clapping. I could do more business with them than I ever could without them. I could've never done this alone, by myself, and knowing that, was more liberating than humbling. And so, it's probably really important for you to know that my main hostess, head waitress, and protective firewall through it all, was my wife Glenda. The love of my life.

And as long as I'm being that honest, you should probably also know that almost all of my best business ideas, or at least major parts of them, were originally hers. But she's never let on about that because I think she wanted me to be successful that bad. But at wild animal shows like these, because we were open on three sides, people were always crowded around the counters eating and watching me cook, but if they wanted anything, had to go thru Glenda first to get anything at all. Glenda could've been a wild animal trainer. One, that could've made the animals actually seem to look forward to obeying her commands. All I had to do is pay attention to what she told me to cook and what the next order was, so I didn't really even have to think; just cook. So, I did.

She handled the surging crowds like a lion tamer, without the chair and whip, everybody got a number, and that, was the order. In a lot of ways, working with your wife in situations like these is better than any program Marriage Encounter could've ever devise. On the other hand, that's why we never went to marriage counseling, we were afraid they'd tell us we deserved each other. We only argued about important things, she continually overlooked the fact that she was my employee, but I continually pretended I could ever do this without her. The main problem being, she knew that I knew that. People around the counters, eating or waiting for food, who knew us, loved to see us have our 'moments' while they ate, it was like dinner theatre to them, kind of like therapy for us. And there were some pretty heated moments and stupid arguments, mostly about whether an order was noodles or rice, or something really important like that.

At lunchtime, precisely the time I feared 'deep wave panic', waves of business we simply couldn't accommodate, my resurrection would occurr. In through the door of our kitchen trailer would bounce our friend and absolute assistant Sheira Atoms.

Her and Glenda and I could take on unbelievable crowds together, with her always saying: 'okeydokey', and somehow making the impossible possible.

Once Sheira arrived, our output capacity tripled, and she worked as if she was reading my mind; she was that good. Shrimp! Chicken! Eggrolls! More shrimp! Like Kirk calling on Scotty for more crystal power. 'You should see the lines of traffic waiting to get in here' she'd tell me, 'this place is going to be a mad house by tonight'. And she was usually right, she knew, she'd worked with us for long enough to know that after the dinner crowd, things always got even wilder and a lot weirder.

Especially at musical events, where attendee's often stayed up, awake and partying for two or three days. You could smell the aroma of enchanted excitement in the air. Everywhere. The energy from their drum circles alone could've probably lit up a string of light bulbs, and, kept it on. All night. Really; bright.

Relief at Sheiras arrival always rejuvenated me in reacquired confidence, like finding yourself adrift after a shipwreck, yet knowing somehow you were going to reach that island on the horizon. Even if, it meant cooking like a crazy person until eleven o'clock that night. I mean, even if it was only a mirage on the horizon, you were at least doing something to save yourself. Ha-ha, I wasn't going to freak out in front of all these strangers after all. Sheira cut my work responsibilities in half while contributing to triple our output. A business degree doesn't seem necessary to explain how something like this could easily influence the way our numbers tumbled. And man, once we got going, our numbers could tumble like a jar full of tumbling dung beetles, or something like that. When the three of us began meshing like gears of the finely tuned machine we were, believe me, our numbers tumbled way into the night, until there were no more crowds until tomorrow. Then, it'd be so quiet you'd hear the peepers, feel the night chill, and smell the lingering vapors of all of that Chinese food. The trailer had a very distinct smell I'll never forget. Pop! Tune back in, Glenda's making her eyes big, excitedly reminding me there's food cooking, and to mess with me, says also, it smells like it's burning. It's her loving way of snapping me back into production mode, cruel, perhaps, necessary, I suppose but she's my wife, my confidant, my employee, my hostess, I smile and redouble my stir frying. She always said stuff like that just to make sure I wasn't having too much fun. That's what I'm remembering now, and smiling about it, about then, but it's what I'm telling you about now. Because even though I'm thinking about then, there, I was thinking about it being here, now. Thinking about it again, all of it. Lying by some stream, in Spain, on a mountain side having finally gotten away, waiting in the crisp morning sunshine for Glenda to arrive with a picnic basket, filled with bottles of wine and food, and I'm clearly remembering the pungent smells of all that Chinese food as if I were still there, at work, at the end of a busy day, remembering myself as feeling as withered and exhausted as an unsold eggroll left over in the deep fryer. Remembering and musing with comic clarity as if it were only yesterday, and feeling nostalgic as if I missed it, but being gladder I wasn't. Lying there, chewing on a piece of grass, I even imagined someone yelling out for chicken lo-mein. Poof! I was a food vendor again. I was there in Spain, on vacation, yet I was there too, back in the middle of food choas. The next band had just taken the stage; with walls of speaker cabinets booming massive vibrating waves of effervescence at the trailer like a sound cannon, making everything shake wildly. Inside, the food pandemonium increased with the tempo of the music. The loudness of it became more of a work place hazard, than enjoyable, making it virtually impossible to hear Glenda shouting orders to me. I could see her lips moving but it seemed she kept saying 'chicken lo- mien' over and over for every order. She is, Sheira told me from behind, stifling laughter. We made literally, tons of chicken lo-mein, it was a speciality, so I shouldn't've been surprised. It went on like this for days at a time, long days, sometimes into longer nights. Sometimes, as I've told you, days after a show was over, someone saying 'chicken lo-mien' to me, could induce symptoms of post-traumatic stress syndrome. Chicken lo-mien was a fabulously popular menu item, but making it two or three hundred times a day was traumatizing.

The craziness of it was electrifying. I could see, but just barely hear Glenda shouting to be heard over the music: '16? 16?! Whose 16? 9, you're up; you want drinks with that? 22's, supposed to be a lo-mien, extra hot peppers no onions...' I look at her with a horrified, bereft look on my face, as I imagine a raccoon looks Nano-seconds before a car squashes him.

'22 is...noodles?' I shout back over super amplified music loudly bouncing off of every surface at the event. Panic sets in. 'No...you're right, 22 is chic- lo, double hot, 23 is 86 onions'. Ahh, catastrophe averted. I felt relieved, saved, vindicated, resurrected. Sheira is once again forcing eggrolls on me; I must be behind I'm thinking, mentally re-checking my status. Mixing up an order really pisses clients off so I made a serious, professional effort not to make rice when I should've been making noodles and vise versa. But, there were moments when stuff like that happened. People, I learned, tend to get really weird about their food, especially if you drop it, even more so, if you pick it up and put it back on their plates using your bare hands. But dropping food because you're hurrying, it in front of them just as you serve it is probably the cruelest joke of all. But hey, in a heavily theatrical food environment like this; stuff just happened from time to time. This, please keep in mind, was like being in an Olympic event, but, one conducted at high speed where more is obviously, better.

So you might sense our motivations for being just as driven. You could actually feel the show heating up, the music getting louder and louder, driving the energy of the crowd into irresistible dance-party mode. The fragrance of ganja was pervasive. But the music would be driving it frenzied, like a drug and alcohol-fueled gathering of stink beetles, all gesturing and gyrating and moving in complete synchronicity with each other. And they danced and partied until exhausted, then worked up their appetites and came looking for us. Lucky me I bet you're thinking, right?

At times like these, it was important to not let yourself begin subconsciously attempting to synchronize cooking with the beat of the music. It happens really subtly until you sense that you're either in a foreign film with bad subtitles or something, or you're actually having that mental break down we talked about earlier.

As a job hazard, it's extremely hard to resist trying to operate faster and faster as the music increases in volume and tempo, you've got to stay completely de-tuned. It was exhilarating beyond belief, incongruous maybe, but something similar to a slightly less lethal version of baptism to combat. You come to realize that if you make it through this, you're never going to be doubtful about anything ever again. I was a wild man; scooping and serving noodles out of one wok, moving smoothly, adding plum sauce to sautéing house special chicken in wok # 2, minding shrimp rice and veggies in wok #3 coming in for a landing. In a highly heated wok, rice is a lot less forgiving than are noodles, and as such, demands much greater cooking vigilance, because in a second, it has the potential to become rice Chernobyl. And that kind of a melt down ain't pretty at all, particularly when the you know what is hitting the fan. To have to stop and detour away from full steam ahead while de-carbonizing one of the woks, is about as bad as a propeller falling off of a ship fighting for stability in a typhoon.

No joke; especially when there's about fifty pairs of eyes watching your every move to see your best impressions of grace under pressure, especially because, or particularly because, you're not even Chinese. This, friends, is one of the ultimate scenario's of grace under pressure. It's so very like a daring final veronica as an insane bull lunges and charges. All the while I'm hearing Glenda yelling '14, 14…you're up. 12…you want those egg rolls on the same platter? That'll be total: twenty-three dollars. 15! 15!…anybody seen 15? …15's MIA!' 'Sell it to someone else', I yell, 'it's still hot isn't it?'

'I'll take it' some voice on my right says, 'I've been standing here watching you cook. Man…how do you do it? I can't see anything that beautiful going to waste; 15's toast, I win.' I hand him 15's order and take his money handing it to Glenda, 'keep the change' he mumbles, stuffing his face using chopsticks.

Suddenly, 15 surfaces, 'you called out my number' 15 explains to Glenda. Bad scenario.

'Glenda' I scream over a fabulous guitar solo, 'tell 15 he's next… we've been looking for him we've been keeping it hot' I lie, keeping all the action in the air going. 'Hold on a minute' Glenda yells, 'what's 17 and 14?' '17 and 14…?' I yell back excitedly, wild-eyed 'that was ages ago…but I think they were both lo-miens…why?'

'No' Glenda screams back over a song about somebodies love for their dog or something, '17 and 14? Oh… 31 never mind…that'll be thirty-one dollars she tells some woman who's squirting a ridiculous amount of duck sauce on a mountain of eggrolls and getting it all over the counter. It was then, in the middle of that pandemonium, that what, do my discriminating sensibilities detect, but the deliciously fragrant aroma of what I've always referred to as 'rock-star' reefer. Capital G ganja, the kind, sinsemilla, crystal girl, what ever you want to call it, and notice some rasta, dread headed dude standing next to me, who wants to know if I 'barter?' and I know exactly what he's got in mind.

'We only take orders in the front' Glenda chastises me like she's got the Napoleon hat on and someone mistakenly left her in charge. 'You stay right there' I tell the Rasta guy, Glenda giving me the look that tells me she knows what's going on. There's no fooling that girl, believe me.

'Just keep cooking' she scolds, reminding me that the order I'm cooking has egg rolls on separate plates. So, that's why Sheira kept offering them to me I suddenly realize, she knew more about what was happening than I did. Acting like I knew what I was doing, I glance at the deep fry basket, panicking at the sight of it being empty.

'I got it' I heard my savior, Sheira say. 'I put the eggrolls in the other basket so I could re-chicken finger the second basket…everything's cool, but we've got six more finger orders up after that, as soon as possible'. I didn't know if we were behind or ahead or even just holding our own and keeping up with all the orders. The ganja guy was still patiently waiting for his barter for noodles, broccoli and hot peppers, but he could see how busy we were and seemed to be actually entertained by it. Besides, Glenda would've flipped out in colors if I started cooking rogue orders on the side, making private deals, out of her sequence. We had an agreed on policy about that kind of thing, she made me promise it wouldn't be done. I kind of agreed, but there were times when I painfully strayed. The guy stood there quietly watching us zoom around like crazed ants, bobbing his head up and down to the music, probably more amazed than entertained. Obviously, pretty baked.

'Those aren't drum sticks honey' Glenda's schoolteacher voice tells some kid back again for more chopsticks. She then turns to Sheira without missing a beat, 'two large iced teas and an Arnold Palmer' (½ tea, ½ lemonade). I watch Sheira's calm demeanor; admiring it, while all food chaos is breaking loose around us, she's actually singing to herself as she works, bobbing her head to her own lyrics. Go figure. Talk about grace under pressure. 'Teas and Palmer up' she tells Glenda calmly as if we weren't busy at all. Man, it's incredibly hot, standing there, working those woks. I feel the spray of atomized sesame oil and rice wine vinegar in my hair and on my skin, one of the downsides to the profession. There are matchsticks of sliced, bright red peppers, that've been squashed into red watery juice on the floor where I stand cooking. Some broccoli florets as well, having been stepped on so many times in the last three hours they're squashed as flat as postage stamps. Suddenly, in the very heart of all this culinary chaos, an extremely large, robust looking woman sidles up next to ganja man, waiting patiently, still, and begins panting desperately, drama queen-like, that she needs the coldest bottle of water I can produce and she needs it, immediately. Like, whoa, stop everything. I can actually feel Glenda giving me 'that' look. The look all husbands come to learn from their wives' over time. The most common response to which, most men, when captured by this look from their wives, at best, comes off like a guilty...'what?' Ganja man seems unperturbed, kind of ignoring his girl friends' lack of patient social grace.

I'm kind of put off, because, for one thing, she's disrespected Glenda's numbering thing, ignoring all the other waiting clients, but she skips off to the side of ganja man, acting like she's expecting to get served before anyone who'd been waiting here since before she showed up. But ganja man has at least been waiting patiently, so not wanting to be rude, maybe spoiling a good opportunity, I tell her, 'Lady...to get a bottle of water that cold, I'd have to run down to the basement to get it...' With the look of the dullest surprise on her face, raises her made up chagrined eyebrows, and asks in all earnest disbelief, 'You've got a basement in there?'

I hear Sheira, behind me, cracking up laughing knowing she'd heard that too. She hands the lady a bottle of water and clinches the sale. I know she's laughing because she still can't believe, after all her time of working with us, the things I'd say to complete strangers. It's how I entertained myself at work. I think of it more as, live, inter-active theatre with unsuspecting participants. And in a lot of ways, that's what it really is, but it's also, so much better, than reality T.V. It's like a real life puppet show where the dialogues are made up at it goes along. Some times more like kabuki theatre, sometime more like theatre of the absurd. Working with Glenda and Sheira has been one of the most special experiences in my life so far. I've worked out some terrific material over the years, using them as my foil. We actually had fun joking and working together, making fun of our travails, about really gullible people and people who just didn't seem or care to seem about 'getting it'.

While Glenda, up front, kept everything running smoothly and efficiently. Believe me, Glenda was worth all of the money she made me pay her, even though, everything usually went to her anyway.

The next band kicks off in high gear, sounding like the heralded second coming channeling Gerry Garcia or something. I'm looking at the clock; bad move. This insane pace has been going on non-stop since opening this morning. My inner self is asking if I feel capable of doing what's going to be required until that night. It could've been the contact high with ganja man, but I found myself in affirmation to bring it on. OK then, game on.

Sheira comes up to me, dutifully handing me two new, unopened fifteen pound bags of noodles. It was just then, four-thirty in the afternoon, and we'd already gone through fourteen, fifteen-pound bags. I quickly computed that that, was, two hundred and ten pounds, leaving only ninety pound more from the three hundred I'd brought this morning, to get through the next several hours. It'd be close I estimated, but felt confident about it, thinking it could very easily be done, that of selling everything we had in stock at the time until there was nothing left to sell at all. The down side was that'd have to be made up again before we opened again in the morning.

Once again, I blip back from my revelries. Glenda is motioning wildly. I'm reading her lips, I can see her asking: 'Can you double chicken those lo- miens, and extra hot the second half of the order?' I know the short hand, and follow her instructions without thinking. Double orders were definitely the way to make money, but they were extremely challenging, mostly because portioning in these cases is everything. One look and people can tell right away if two plates appear as similar as possible. You can easily mess up someone's mind if you give them way too much food, almost as much as you can, if you don't give them what their eyes tell them, isn't enough. So, learning to deliver reasonably proportioned amounts of food became an absolute rule. But a double or triple order in the same wok was definitely the way money was made. It translates into cooking two, four, or six orders at the same time. You could almost hear the sales chinging up as the totals increased. And that's a very pleasing sound, the sound of money being made. The drummer begins pounding out a solo driven with the frenzied driving beat of a run-away locomotive; I can only liken it to the rampaging sounds of a bunch of Yaks about to stampede, I mean, I'm trying to cook. The drums are so mic'ed up; the crescendo loudly crashes from the wall of speaker cabinets sounding like machine gun fire, or the launch pad at Cape Canaveral during blast off. It's deafening, even the people dancing up front are holding their hands over their ears. It ain't over yet though, as Glenda turns to me like a Stepford waitress yelling: 'double chic lo, double rolls, triple cold nudes'.

'I'm on it' Sheira confirms handing three orders of cold sesame noodles with peanut sauce to Glenda. How does she do that? And, I hear she's still quietly singing to herself…go figure. I find I'm staring vacantly at the tip jar on our counter. I see, besides lots and lots of ones, some fives, a couple of tens, and I think…even a twenty-dollar bill. I'm flattered but don't let myself get too excited. At rock shows like these, lots and lots of funny money showed up, all the time. And every time we'd give out change for like an egg roll or something, they always seemed to pay with a twenty-dollar bill; we'd be giving back real money for funny money in return. It's a totally anonymous, no loose proposition for the people doing the con all over the event, but in the crush of the moment there's virtually nothing anyone can do about it. It's like finding quicksand by falling in it. It's a calculated dangle on an old angle. Sometimes the person doing the short con would, over the course of two days, buy many egg rolls, but because we'd never know who; would flood us with wads of worthless Monopoly money. It makes you feel you can't trust anybody, and that's not such a great feeling.

Amazingly, there's a brief window of respite around five-thirty, before the dinner crowd crush begins.

I'm exhausted, and turning, see the ganja guy's still there, unbelievably, still bobbing his head up and down to the music.

'Wow' he says, sounding baked to perfection, 'I never been in a Chinese kitchen before...it's...awesome...it was totally exciting, how much do I owe you for my order?' I looked at Sheira, raising my eyebrows, she begins laughing, realizing I hadn't even made it for him yet. I wasn't sure if he even realized it, or thought he'd eaten it already, or who at that point was more baked, him, or me.

This is how I learned using my faux-pas imperfections to best advantage. This, I learned is one successful way of crowd sourcing return customers. I look at ganja man standing there bobbing and smiling, and tell him 'you've been so patient, so right now, anything you want, anything, is on me'. Suddenly, I've got his completely rapt attention. 'Really?' he asks incredulously. 'Really' I tell him, 'pay no attention to anything my wife says...' I noticed him steal a quick glance at Glenda without making eye contact, as if checking out if it really was OK. 'Well, I'll take a house special lo-mien then, and make it really hot'. 'Well how hot do you want it brother?' I ask him, 'I can really melt you down if that's what you want...' 'Then, send me to the hospital' he says from under heavy eyelids. I'm surprised I didn't kill the guy, I knew how to really spice things up, but he ate it all, and, wanted more! As he said this, I noticed him opening a little leather pouch from around his neck, and shaking out what he intended bartering with. To me, it looked like a win-win arrangement for both of us, and Sheira as well. I heard her exhale loudly, 'oh my God' and saw her rolling her eyes. She knew what I had going on, and knew also because of that, I'd share with her later. This time, I looked forcefully at Glenda, certain she was intentionally ignoring what I had going on, but Sheira hadn't missed a thing. I looked at Sheira, innocently dropping more egg rolls as she looked at me and began laughing. 'Share-zies after the show' I told her, 'I promise', she just smiled. She really loved where she worked, we paid her more than she'd ever earned before in her life, and offered plenty of odd fringe benefits, like this, but I knew she loved us for more than just that. I considered it, as taking care of my people; she considered it as loving where she worked.

The shows M.C. came on stage again announcing the evening musical line ups, asking if everybody was having fun, and reminding everyone again, of the other vendors, again, without saying 'besides the Chinese people'. But it didn't matter, because at that point in the program, I sensed that I'd become one of the sacred vending elders myself, and everything was going to work out, somehow, it always had up to this point. I smiled to myself and thought, 'bring on the dinner crowd'. I got my second wind.

And just like that; lines began queuing up again just like all day long. Wild-eyed in panic, Glenda began frantically motioning to me while her mouth was full of Arnold Palmer, gesticulating excitedly for me to pay attention and see what she was seeing. I feared at first that I'd left a wok burning on high, and it wouldn't have been the first time. I followed her shaking, pointing finger and came to see what she was so frantic about. There, outside the trailer, on the table used as our supply table, where our five-gallon containers of fresh water were stored for more tea or lemonade was something I couldn't believe I was seeing at all.

With the lid off of one of the water containers, a reasonably intelligent looking woman, perhaps in her younger thirties, obviously monstrously inebriated, almost naked from the waist up except for her brasizzare, washing her shirt in my lemonade water.

The band was playing loud enough to be heard in Europe. I was so blown away watching this woman; all I could blurt out was a panicky version of 'WTF are you doing?' The woman, stood there wobbling around in circles, looking at me with half closed eyes, swaying around like she was on a ride, wringing her shirt out, back into my water container.

Sheira so paralyzed with laughter; tears were streaming from her eyes actually crying. 'My boy friend said it'd be OK' she slobbered as an explanation. 'I'll handle it Sheira says. When I paid attention back inside the trailer, I could see Glenda motioning hysterically to begin cooking again. Dinnertime, there was an enormous line forming. By the time I'm repositioned at my battle station, I'm already behind three orders. The sun is going down, mellow folk rock begins taking the edge off of an intense after noon and I know I can easily make it to the end. I'm feeling snarky. Feeling like I'd just spent the afternoon treading water in the shark tank at feeding time. Now, I'm feeling hopeful, knowing it's been a good day. Especially, after my bartering session with ganja guy, I felt I had something to look forward to, a reward for persevering. Something to look forward to...what's better than that? I look up from cooking, there's a guy standing silently to my right, pointing, and staring at me. He's got his arm around the shoulders of a naked woman dressed only in blue and silver glitter as a giant butterfly with lots of glitter covering her essential parts and little gauzy wings on and not much of anything else. She's staring too, real wide eyed, from some distant galaxy. I look back at him realizing who he is. He's the guy who was here earlier, with no money, the one who I'd fed earlier for free. He was back. With a butterfly? I could hear him telling the butterfly, '...this is the Chinese guy I told you about'. 'He doesn't look too Chinese to me...' the butterfly says.

'That's the beauty of what he's doing' the guy tells her; 'he isn't.' 'I don't get it' the butterfly says, 'He isn't Chinese? I don't get it'. He'd come back to pay me, and bought the butterfly some noodles too, she loved them, ate them all and gave us our biggest tip of the day. From a butterfly. He'd come back because, as always, whenever I gave away free food, I knew there never was, or ever will be as an effective sales pitch as the 'free give away'. The only thing I ever requested from people I fed for free, was that if they ever found themselves coming back to pay us; to bring their hungry friends. No joke, that little tactic, made lots of sales over twenty-five years and all that, adds up to something. But it wasn't always as easy as this. It was the learning curve that'd brought me here to where I found myself that made it so interesting. And there were no guardrails on most of those curves. But I never would've imagined I ever would've ended up here, daydreaming about all that, by a stream in the cordillera Penibetica, in Spain, waiting for Glenda and her lunch basket after such humble beginnings.

As the next band began tearing up the stage I find myself thinking, here we go again and began remembering cooking to save myself. Wondering where I'd go if I could escape all of this, just to think about it all.

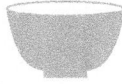

CHAPTER 2

'MAIDEN VOYAGES'

All those times I found myself cooking as fast as I could, often, all day and late into the night, the only thing that kept me sane was imagining where I'd go when I couldn't stand being successful any longer. And believe me, I was working hard at being successful too; the problem I suspected, maybe, was working too hard at it. I imagined I'd escape, to a place where no one ever thought of saying 'chicken lo-mien'. I imagined it to be a mild, sunny place with abundantly open, mountain like nothingness. And then, one day I found myself there. High up in the Cordillera Penibetica, north of Granada Spain, hovering in the clouds above the Costa del Sol. It was almost as I had imagined it, dreaming about it for so long, over and over. Its' rugged beauty reminded me of every Hemingway description about the beauty of Spain. It was a place I felt I could happily remain carefree for the rest of my life. So, I'm lying there in the warm, early morning Spanish sun trying to forget about wondering when I began first feeling I'd lost control of my life; and at that point, a bunged up little car with four overweight guys passing around a bottle in it goes jostling by. Bouncing up and bottoming out with grunts and scrapes through the field. Their laughter and singing burst out the open windows, all singing and partying. A car! Completely breaks my concentration, causes me to fall out of Nirvana like a piano. A car, I'm thinking to myself, a car, in the absolute middle of nowhere. I mean, I'm in a place where it'd be difficult to go on a burrow, and suddenly, I'm back to where, I started from. Squinching eyes closed tighter, trying to ignore it, my mind begins focusing instead on the endlessly murmuring stream, so soothing that it lulls me into a languid state of nothingness, floating above scenes from my childhood. 'That; was a pretty chaotic period for me', I hear my mind reaffirm; 'back in the early days, the formative days'. Adults, back then, seemed only to say things like, 'shut up, sit down, that's stupid, who told you that? Or, there's no such thing', and that, I supposed, was supposed to be that.

What did I know? Back then I was just a kid trying to figure out anything about how girls or the world, worked.

Especially girls. Girls to me at that point were so beyond being something else that my uncertainty about myself must have been obvious to them. On the other hand, I was a lot more concerned about understanding myself and what was really going on; not only about myself, but the world around me. I knew too, that as soon as I graduated from school, I'd be drafted into a war I was fervently opposed to. Satisfying answers were less than forth coming from newspapers, magazines, teachers, and adults in general, or Boy scouts, and, forget entirely about politicians. I remembered being that young and wondering who you could believe about anything? So in an attempt to find answers about anything, I let myself, as a kid, be convinced that maybe those answers had something to do with religion.

Big mistake. Look, it's wonderful to have faith in something, to believe in things that are greater than yourself. It's fine to believe in things you can't see or prove; but it's also called 'slight of hand', which requires only believing, especially in things you can't see or prove. Has it ever seemed to you that humans readily suspend their disbelief simply to have something they can believe in at all? Is it just me that finds that a bit curious? So, I'd caution you about letting yourself get talked into anything that requires the absolute suspension of disbelief. I'm sorry if I'm destroying anyone's belief in the tooth fairy, or the Easter Bunny, that's not my intent. I can only suppose you would've found out for yourself, eventually. Whether or not you believed it was another issue entirely. But the hardest, most confounding part about that bit of advice; is to caution you also, to not believe or disbelieve anything too entirely. After all, there really are things that happen, things that just can't be explained or proven. Ain't that just like life? So maybe believing in anything; also means keeping an open mind about other possible explanations about the same things. I've had direct personal experiences like these I still can't explain to myself, and yet, they happened, changing my life forever. I just stopped wondering about why things happened, happened at all, and began letting myself become convinced that life, at times, for whatever reasons, is just curious and wonderful. Most of the answers I was looking for at those times though; seemed only to be found by explaining things to myself. But true changes, come only from within. Right?

For example, the only way for explaining my parents' behavior back then, is to suppose they'd apparently decided I needed religion in my life. A lot more than they did, a lot more than I even knew I needed myself.

It was therefore mandatory every Sunday, for me to attend Sunday school, and, church afterwards, every Sunday. Before long, I began suspecting I was hearing versions of the same stories over and over until I felt I knew them all by heart. It seemed everything was about either right or wrong, or knowing the sins and differences between and their consequences. All the fun stuff seemed to be off limits, and at the time, it was all pretty confusing. Virtually every adult I observed back then, seemed to be doing or believing all the stuff I was being told was sinfully off limits. I considered maybe that's why they always said that 'vice was nice' because fewer words rhymed with religious, moral or ethical. The more those weekly sermons seemed to drone on, the more I drifted off into the realm of my own little thoughts about God and what God really is, or was, or might be. I thought about that a lot, and started realizing I couldn't prove or disprove God; I just had to believe.

Mostly, I spent time trying to imagine anything greater than God, who seemed, after all those sermons, as being, everything. And so, I simply began thinking of God as 'anything and everything' because I just couldn't think of, or imagine, anything greater than anything, and it seemed almost indescribable, trying to imagine something that was beyond everything at all? What those sermons really made me wonder about; was what happened when life ended? Even I had figured out that everything that lives, comes to an end, everything. I realized it wasn't a question of 'if', only of 'when and how'. And my young mind wondered about that, a lot, about facing God on that day, and having to explain how I used the wonderful gift of my life. It all made me feel so tiny and pointless. I decided then, that if God were a forgiving God, not a vengeful one, he'd smile and forgive me, but probably make me watch secretly recorded video taped highlights of my life that he'd recorded. Those, I knew, would be the hardest part because they would've most likely showed me freaking out over something as stupid as stepping in dog shit and being completely human about it. Thinking about that, enabled me to determine attempting to live with a sense of calm, patient atonement. Keeping in mind that any day could be the last, and the very last thing I ever wanted for myself was to have to watch replays of me freaking out over dog shit in the presence of God.

The best way for avoiding that, I resolved; was trying always, to do the right thing. The thing that'd bring peace of mind, because I knew I'd done what I knew to be the right thing to do. Because on that fateful day, there'll be no more pretending, that day is when the accounting begins. On that day, whatever shall be; shall be, and I don't mean any que sera, sera either. On that fateful day it'll be too late for confessing anything, and even less meaningless, if that's possible, begging for forgiveness. So do the right thing.

What's the right thing? Look, everyone knows people act differently if they suspect they're being watched, and worse if they think no one's watching at all, and even worse if they think they can do something and get away with it without anyone knowing or seeing. They're only fooling themselves. Because knowing the right thing is about knowing yourself, liking who you are, because that's why you're like that. What we're talking about is, peace of mind. I decided that instead of searching the sky for a role model, I'd try to find one here, on earth. I needed a role model, one that would help me with the consequences of my actions and leave me feeling good about myself and the choices I'd made.

Maybe it was because I was so impressionable, but when inspiration finally arrived, it altered the course of my life. Mahatma Gandhi counseling his followers once said 'they should become the changes they seek in the world'. That, to my young mind, seemed a noble, productive and purposeful way of living life while in pursuit of the changes I sought in the world. I would, I thought to myself, become those changes. However, the moment I began living as Gandhi would have me do, I ran into trouble, making myself an easy target, especially by people I considered to have daunted courage and even less imagination.

Eyebrows raised authoritatively, those, I was taught to respect believing they 'knew better', disparaged that though he did, good, Gandhi was primarily a troublemaker not content to just let things be. Apparently, his faults were, that he not only didn't know his place, he wasn't content to be in it either. That made him seem like my kind of guy.

Admittedly, he certainly had an impact on people, but loved or hated, people just love to talk trash about anyone trying to do anything. Particularly about anyone trying to create changes rather than continuing to do things the same old way and being satisfied with getting the same old results, over and over. Consider that it takes a lot of courage to go around rabble rousing in a diaper wearing skinny little wire glasses and sandals, but that, was Gandhi's schtick. It seems as ridiculous as doing stand up comedy wearing nothing but a sock on your penis and pretending it's not there at all, but, hey, if it gets results, that means it's working.

Either way, venerated or disparaged, he used life as his message for change, not just for himself, but for everyone. He knew what the right thing was, and acted on it. Contrast this with other notables who also knew what the right thing was, and ignored it completely for their own rewards, Pol Pot, Hitler, Henry Kissinger, Pinochet, Richard Nixon, Baby Doc, Idi Amin, it's a pretty long, pathetic list.

The truth remains though, even today; Gandhi was a believing little hipster with a faith you didn't want to mess with. Using life as his weapon of choice and consciousness as the voice of fairness and good, he left the world a better place than the one he was born into. Besides, who wanted to be remembered as the one who hit a skinny little guy wearing glasses and a diaper who wouldn't fight back? To my thinking, Gandhi's ideas were more than just cool; they inspired how to practically apply life in creating and effecting changes in reality. I felt I just couldn't live with the same old moral imperatives over and over until I died.

Please, understand, I never meant to change the world, only to create a personal code I could abide by, like the 'Dude', and with any luck, bring in a little daily bread while doing what needed getting done. Obviously, college wasn't for me, any more than was getting religion or some shill-like corporate job. I felt the overwhelming need for creating something of my own, an alternate universe I could live in. One I wanted to live in. But first, it all had to be clear in my mind. You cannot benefit from a dream you don't yourself, believe in. The next challenge was acting out my dreams in the real world and make them work.

One of my personal mottos is, have fun. When something stops being fun, why continue doing it? I wanted to do something fun that was so real; it seemed almost unreal that I was doing it at all. The adventure began as a lucratively bizarre business education and ended as an incredible life experience.

Or; at least, up until to now, I found myself thinking. Remember, I'm imagining and remembering all this while lying in the sun along some stream in Spain. And I'm wondering, whether or not a movie about my life would be boring? I mean would I be satisfied with my own explanations of anything? I recalled thinking about why you should never explain yourself. The people who need to hear it most likely won't believe you, and the people who don't need to hear it…well…don't need to hear it.

In any event, not being true to myself made me feel like Gumby after shock treatments, having not only not benefited from that modality of treatment, but getting progressively more and more burned out until he was nothing but burnt gum. I couldn't go there. I wanted to live. I wanted to catch a wave and ride it, having fun, all the way into the beach. I needed something I could believe in for sure, not something everybody took somebody else's' word for.

What I needed, I decided, was to get my own game going, and learn to play it better than anyone else.

I could feel myself smiling. Remember, I'm lying there in the sun in Spain, recalling the day I realized the change I wanted to create in the world. My young purpose, at that point, seemed to have had finally arrived. My dedication was going to be working to end stupidity. And I was going to do it using food, by creating alternative festival food really worth buying, really nutritious to eat and healthy for you in many other ways as well. So, I'm lying there, listening to the stream, feeling good about deciding to have finally escape and suddenly, I'm hearing myself thinking… 'It just stopped being fun any longer'. Why do anything that isn't fun? Unless you're like one of those people who turn themselves in for crimes they didn't even commit. Forcefully ignoring any intention for considering it any further, guess what? My mind begins nostalgically drifting back to memories of the beginning, the early days.

Then, believe it or not, I'm suddenly feeling helplessly wistful, wishing those early days could've stayed that way forever. Not only that, but now seeing clearly that at some point, everything had to end and change. Everything always has to. Even me. Especially me. I just couldn't go on any longer, I'd lost my joy, and it began making me feel just like being at work. It had to have a finale, but at the beginning I wasn't thinking about the ending. In the beginning I was more interested in flying and soaring than crashing. In the beginning of anything, the exhilarated excitement of flying and soaring makes things as important and simple as, landing for example, easily overlooked. Actually, crashing and burning can be pretty instructive as well. But how many times has it ever been said, that there's never any place better for beginning anything, than at the beginning?

It occurred to me, lying there, stretched out on some rocks, that, that's exactly why those early days were so exciting.

Every day meant learning new things, solving problems as I went along, making up whatever worked and faking the rest. I never thought I'd miss all of that, but looking back on it, made it now seem like a lot of fun.

Man, I got to wear a lot of different hats back then, it was an unusual adventure, believe me. I believed in what I was doing more than ever before, and was about to unleash it upon the world. It made me wonder what Gandhi would've vended.

Seems pretty much everything you do in life is based upon what you believe. Therefore, I should tell you I believe that you become what you do. And the more and the longer you do it, the more you become it, until it finally becomes you. I wanted to find my niche. One of my greatest fears is to go through life feeling I've never found my niche. And I've hungered for that niche like a drunken stooge. This should give you a pretty clear picture of everything I had in mind and how I intended to pull it off. One of my biggest mistakes back then, was thinking I could ever do it alone, by myself. I hadn't yet realized that everything has its learning curve and requires time to discover. And those learning curves have no guardrails to keep you from going over the edge. But learning about how hard it is to find good help became no longer a joke. Combating stupidity by marketing affordable dietary alternatives seemed too good an opportunity to pass up and really, didn't seem that crazy to me. No one else was doing it, at least, not at the time; I'd never seen a Chinese take out at any event or festival. I saw it as a potentially profitable, novel, niche business market. I could give it just the right amount of schtick to make it work, and only had to sell a small amount of noodles, rice and veggies and such, to make a small investment quite worthwhile. Wow! I was liking this idea more and more as I thought it through, and about what I needed to do to make it work.

It was this basic in the beginning, simple is good, right? Simple is easy, right? Well, not necessarily, but it'd require some doing before I learned the lesson that things that look easy, usually aren't. The motivation for working as hard as this was obviously going to require, was based on the plan to only work six months of the year. I mean, really, who believes going to work everyday is a blessing in disguise? Unless you're one of those people who can't get enough of something, but I'm not one of them. I simply wanted more time to do the things I wanted to do, and going to work everyday wasn't one of them. Besides, most of the things I love doing wouldn't make me capable of producing income, cooking was something I loved, and felt I could do profitably. But where does one begin such a journey? At the beginning was my best guess; I guess it was just a lucky one.

I began by reading cookbooks. Lots of cookbooks, and they made me realize how much I had to learn to make what I was about to do to earn an income, look easy. Forget about being any good at it, I was on a mission; there was no turning back.

I usually read the last pages of books first, to determine if I've got what it takes to read them all the way through. You can't do that with cookbooks. Fortunately, books are my favorite food; I might even be an over-eater. What I'm getting at, is that 'getting there' in getting anywhere at all, is what the trip is all about. Arrival is merely the conclusion to everything required to get there, wherever 'there' happens to be. Getting there; is like the last pages in a book, reading it is how you get there. It's why I read books through to the end; it's a process I know that works. So, there it was in a nutshell. Just thinking about it seemed a little overwhelming, but frightening in a fun way.

From the very beginning my work was cut out for me. Learning to cook, build a vending trailer, do wiring and plumbing, do marketing, be head mechanic, take charge of advertising, head up purchasing products, do public relations with the people I wanted to have include me in their events and generally, figure it all out as I went along. Whatever it took to work seemed to make the rest of it make sense and seem possible. Had anyone asked me if I knew how to run a 'high speed digitally controlled reflecting deep space telescope', I would've said, 'sure, doesn't everyone?' Fortunately, no one's ever asked me, and I'll gladly tell you why. I'm trying to be true to myself, to get through life, without lying, and though at times it's hard to do the 'right thing', it's harder living with myself, knowing I didn't when I had the chance to.

Doing the right things create changes, actually empowering you. But it's even harder to live with yourself for not doing what you know is right, at the right time, and instead, living with regret. Doing the 'right thing' builds character not only because it's the right thing to do, but; because it makes you become who you are in the future. And you become that way because that's the way you are, not because somebody might be watching you, (and you never really know if there is), or even if because there might be. Even if you're only scrutinizing your own consciousness, everyone wants peace of mind right? Easiest way of getting that; is by 'doing the right thing', every time you can, and taking the rest off your mind. The result: joy and happiness almost too good to believe.

Listen, you owe it to yourself to pay attention to what's going on in your life. It's one of the best things you can do for yourself. That, and wondering about the future is healthy, and; it's the one thing you can be sure of that'll be here before you know it. So realizing this, I began seeing myself in the future as being successful, but willing to work hard at it too, and believing it could be possible as well, but not only in a monetary sense. I became an entrepreneur.

Seriously, I convinced myself this, was all leading somewhere in the future that'd be good for me, the problem was having no clue as to where. It simply became what I did to earn my daily bread without having to go to work everyday. And oddly enough, the more I did it, the better it seemed to go, and be fun, until it began taking on a life of it's own. And though I was working longer and harder than at a regular job, it was mine, I was the very cutting edge of my own self-discovery. Man, I tell you, it felt like I was on a roll, and everybody knows, you never quit when you're on a roll, especially if you're a bit ahead of where you started from, and things are going good. I began believing that whenever whatever could happen, happened; I'd adapt and benefit from it if I could, but leave myself wide open to wonder occurring, because I believed it would. I actually believed that; like I was willing it to happen, and still do believe wonder, eventually, always happens. Then, that's exactly what began occurring.

Inspiration came from another motto, 'live right to be right'. Admit it, at some point; it becomes meaningless to wonder WTF is going on. Your guess on that; is about as good as mine, but it kind of leaves you hoping you've done the right thing all along. Right? The hardest part about believing anything, is figuring out what you believe about anything. After that, wondering how an ant goes about moving a mountain is nothing, why; an ant would ever want to move a mountain in the first place hadn't yet even occurred to me.

CHAPTER 3

'MOVING MOUNTAINS'

I realized the fruits of ones' own labor are much sweeter, just harder to get at and felt much better about finally making a life changing decision. One that was going to change my life, because that's the pay off for working that hard, but thinking about it was like comtemplating moving a mountain. I was staggered by not even knowing where to begin. I was the ant. Moving that mountain began by the ant first building the vending trailer. Having never before, done anything like that got it built by imagining what would be needed to do everything on location, our own water, power, fuel, food. The finished product was beautifully impractical, tiny, a bit top heavy, and kind of wobbly having only a single axel; and came out looking like a giant birdhouse or Punch and Judy stand on wheels.

To celebrate and try it out at home, we threw a party we billed as the 'Happy 80th Birthday Grandma' party so the neighbors wouldn't call the police, especially because we intended fireworks. After that we were launching into our first summer of vending with a bizarre non-sequitor line up of shows. Flea markets, bicycle races, craft shows, jazz concerts, horse shoeing contests, anywhere I could get us booked in, you'd find us there. We christened that trailer the 'Punch and Judy' trailer because of its' shape and size, with only one large opening for vending from that really made it look like a 'Punch and Judy' stage. Even more so when we were in it working like two, crazed life sized marionetts arguing about rice or something equally ridiculous, learning our craft, making our bones and honing our skills. Until then, it never occurred to us how we appeared to our client-market-audience, hadn't even occurred to us at all, or been considered. But let me tell you, appearances, we came to learn, count for everything about confirming reality, especially along the lines of, 'if it walks like a duck, and quacks like a duck... Honestly, the whole Punch and Judy set up made people very curious. Our amateurish homemade signage announced we were selling Chinese food and it certainly smelled kind of like it, drawing in crowds. But once they got close and saw two very not very Chinese people cooking what looked like Chinese food, it was immediately pretty obvious we weren't Chinese at all, and that baffled a lot of potential clients. An elderly Chinese man was standing there, in front of our 'stand' reading our signage, trying to decipher our made up Chinese characters, questioning me with a disclaiming, squinting face asking 'What say? Say nothing!' shaking his head soberly, like he'd been hit on it by a rock, and walked away talking to himself, laughing and shaking his head, making me realize the potential of advertising in other languages. By our next show we had authentic Chinese characters advertising our menu. They promised, 'fresh vegetables from the garden, eaten with rice or noodles' and we were the only vendors on any lot that advertised in other languages.

Besides just not being not Chinese, not being Chinese created a mystified confusion in what people were seeing compared to what they were expecting to see. Especially with all the other vendors and everyone else on the 'lot' continuously referring to us as the 'Chinese people'. Also, we were kind of an anomoly because we really weren't Chinese and were usually set off and apart in some obscure section of everything going on, and still, people wandered in from smelling our food cooking. We thought it was kind of funny, even considering it to be an ironic selling point. We looked like large animated puppets in aprons, fumbling around on a tiny stage, making a mess with rice and noodles and such. We were totally faking it with every dish we served, trying to make every dish look exactly the same, you can't imagine how hard that is to learn. Making it up as we went along, finding out what worked and what didn't. In the early days, more than once I was asked if I thought what I'd just cooked and served looked Chinese to me. I'd follow their eyes down, both of us looking at the food and then plummet head first from the top floor of my idealism to the basement, bursting on impact and exploding like a meat bomb, making me feel as if I might be sick. Right away it became apparent that people had expectations of us, based on what they saw, and of course, what they smelled cooking. And what they saw first and foremost, was that I wasn't Chinese (and neither was Glenda for that matter), therefore; how could this be Chinese food? I looked upon this bit of experiential providence as knowledge. I was learning that conjouring magic's not so much about pulling rabbits out of a hat, as it is about putting magic in the 'schtick'.

I suppose knowning that; should've been some kind of a sign of things to come, but it wasn't. To me, all it meant was, more learning curve. Yet, it was still, an important sign along that curve that spoke to me about future possibilities. I'm a big believer in signs and symbols, but, I really believe, in 'schtick', and I know how difficult it is to walk the talk. Talking the talk is cheap; I had to learn to believe in myself, and do what I dreamed of doing, confidently and unafraid to let people see my moves. I knew I wasn't Chinese. So what? At the time, whether or not, I was, or wasn't Chinese hadn't even occurred to me, didn't even matter. I only knew I had nothing to prove to anyone, but myself. Take my word; until you challenge yourself, and know what it's like to do the shim sham shuffel in one form or another trying to make a living, you ain't done nothin'. I was building connections between all kinds of people one plate of noodles at a time, and with the simple love of doing it at all, I was doing something.

Doing something actively, living the dream, being the power and imagination behind making it all happen. And, beginning to make money doing it too; even beginning to feel good about being the Chinese guy, if that's what it took. And apparently, becoming the 'Chinese' guy seemed to have something that 'clicked' about marketing.

Everyone came to know that the Chinese guy had a fabulous work ethic, first vendor open, last one to close at night. Asian clients claimed he even cooked better than their mothers. And I happen to know, that when that guy who wasn't Chinese heard that, his mind began sizzling, imaginging accepting the coveted, crossed, golden ginzu knives mounted on a faux marble pedestal, the most prestigously recognized rice, and noodle merchants accolade attainable. Let me tell you, I really believed I was becoming something by doing something, but I never would've guessed it would ever be becoming being not Chinese, but, hey, so be it. Everything is what it is, until it isn't any longer, but this, made me determined to succeed. I was unafraid of failing. I was unafraid of making myself an easy target for cheesey remarks. I was becoming part of everything about my life, everything about my life, was becoming a part of me. Weird how stuff happens huh? I began realizing I was becoming part of all the people who believed in me, by becoming a part of all of their lives, achieving recognition as a real life 'Zelig', a total social chameleon, but a successful chameleon. To everyone else I became the Chinese guy, but to myself I was becoming more real. I was seeing my own effect upon the world. This then, is the substance of my tale. Of all the people, who, over time, supported and enabled my success, thereby shaping my life, enabling me to become who I am, as well as to achieve an understanding, that love, joy friendship and success, always triumph over deceit, greed, and avariciousness. When I was a kid, it seemed everyone was telling me I'd never be anything, and I fought against seeing myself that way because I was something. I was alive, and now, I was making 'something' of myself. Sure, I could've been a Dentist, or a Lawyer, or a fireman, or, maybe even a successful criminal if I had wanted to, but apparently I didn't. So when I recognized the opportunity to be successful, I became Chinese. Weird huh? Even weirder is, that even as being not a Chinese guy being Chinese, I became reasonably successful in the process. What was important was getting comfortable with believing that 'what shall be, shall be', never knowing what'll happen next, learning to trust in a higher power. Not knowing what'll happen next in life is like what I imagine God to be. Something you're never completely certain about, because with God, you can never really sure. You've got to operate more on faith, and hope Gods camera isn't running. But not knowing the future is definitely the greatest wonder of life. Stuff just, happens. I was living with the choices I was making about my life. As odd as that sounds, maybe it was just my fate to end up as not Chinese after working that hard, who can ever know? OK, so we weren't Chinese, therefore, how could we be not Chinese and be selling Chinese food? More learning curve about marketing product was obvious, guardrails or not. At first it escaped my comprehension about why people expected me to be Chinese to be a good Chinese cook when it was so obvious I was just a good cook who wasn't Chinese.

But this became the spiritual mission of marketing, that of not being one thing, while entirely being something else. I was just a tiny part of this greater adventure taking shape as, my life occurring. It made me feel like Siddhartha wanting to be more like Huck Finn. But you've got to do what you've got to do, and I decided that if I had to, I'd be Siddhartha going down the Mississippi on a raft with Tom Sawyer and Huck Finn, but no diapers, which in a lot of ways seemed to be pretty much the same thing as not being Chinese.

What I loved most about a career vending was, never knowing what would happen at any given moment. But, it was the concept of using a trailer for doing business in any location that was key. The idea wasn't new, but it was new to me; it was a case of Mohammed, going to the freaking mountain; after realizing the mountain wasn't coming to him, that's all. This single aspect of marketing from a mobile location alone, eliminated the need for relying on the volumes of foot traffic a successful business requires. Using the trailer meant no fixed overhead expenses either, like mortgage or rent for a place to do business in; we owned its' location wherever it was. But the best part of the trailer was that it could go anywhere we needed to be, wherever that hungry foot traffic was.

Our business location could be changed at any time using a trailer; that was really important. Being so tiny was important as well too, but not for long. Renting spots at events at the time was generally calculated as so many dollars per square foot of needed space, utilities and so many feet of frontage. In this case, tiny was good for obvious reasons. Most eating-places go under because of, either cash flow, or lack of foot traffic, which means cash flow in different words. Major location over-head issues, or some fatal combination therein are the undoing of many food joints, particularly ones with fixed locations. The unforeseen problem for us, as new guys, was almost always, one of location. Our newness to the business, and the obviously homemade, unflashy appearance of our trailer usually got us situated in the most undesirable and least advantageous spots. The long timers and vending elders didn't want any unnecessary disruption or competition to their acquired monetary prestige. They were battling it out between themselves slinging the same old greasy sausage, burger, deep-fried, smothered in onions kind of stuff they'd been slinging since they began, why change? And in the middle of all this, is suddenly some nut selling vegetarian health food? Not likely! So we often ended up in dead end side lanes, or behind sheep barns, under bleachers, or tucked away somewhere where the only people walking by were usually going to the bathrooms wondering why we were set up in such a hidden location. Being new meant playing against established players with big fancy trailers all decked out with flags and colored banners flapping and snapping in the wind, with flashing lights going on and off everywhere, and, in the best locations because they'd been there for the last twenty or thirty years and knew what locations were the best.

So that's why, as guerilla vendors, we sought out weird little gems of shows that'd be thrilled to have any vendor to serve their crowds at all. This, is where the weirdness really began happening.

While trying to solve the conundrum of location, we were also beginning to figure out exactly who our buying audience was, and how important it was to know where those audiences went. Figuring that out, would lead to doing only shows where they'd likely be found. Until those insights were gained however, destiny and necessity required us to try many different events, endlessly looking for them. Searching them out, hence, going on safari. It was really weird; the shows we did, the shows that did us. It was like a little bird learning to fly by crashing and bumping along on the ground. This learning curve we were on had no guardrails or warning signs. Baby, you were on your own. Bust or win, make it or break it, the game was on and zooming around those curves at high speed made me feel dare devilishly joyful, as if I were playing high stakes poker with Monopoly money and needed to keep a cool, confidant, straight faced and not burst out laughing. It was my mistake; I thought to be successful I had to pretend to be Chinese even though I wasn't to be believable.

On the other hand not being Chinese turned out way better than I ever guessed it would. In fact, only the food had to be Chinese. Even though I wasn't, the food definitely had to be, it was what everyone expected. What I was providing, was an option that enabled people to experience being the changes they, sought for themselves in the world. I had to believe I could do at least that. I had to believe I could be part of a paradigm shift I believed in. Otherwise, it meant I was full of shit, and never should've let myself believe otherwise. After all, talking the talk would be unbelievably meaningless to anyone who needed to hear it, and unnecessarily meaningless to anyone who didn't need to hear it, or didn't care. So, I stopped talking the talk, realizing I had nothing to prove to anyone except myself. Then, began struggling to walk the talk instead. That's like volunteering for interaction with the future with no firm idea of what that's all about, or what the outcome is likely to be. It's just using ideas about life as a roadmap into things that haven't happened yet because they're still in the future. That doesn't have to be talked about, just acted upon. Talking the talk is always easier than walking the walk, but walking the talk, is the adventure it leads you on, and makes all the difference in the world, whether you're Chinese or not.

But, the trailer; man, we could go anywhere there was business to be done; and so we did. Every weekend fostered the creation of another adventure in the guerilla-vending field hand book. We thought of it, and talked about it, as 'going out on an operation'. In those early years, we hauled that goofy little trailer everywhere, traveling all over New England, every weekend. Looking for any show that'd book us in. Not yet having identified our target market, our client profile, everything had to be considered possible; tattoo festivals, dog shows, hand made boat shows, anything, anywhere, and we left very few stones unturned. We booked boat shows, dog shows, car shows, home shows, tattoo festivals, carnivals, local and state fairs, reggae concerts, street fairs, antique festivals, art shows, craft shows, 4H events, Harley Davidson swap meets, demolition derbies, holistic health shows, jazz concerts, home-made boat shows, medieval and civil war re-enactments, goat and sheep shows, rock and roll events, Indian Pow-Wow's, horse shows, bicycle races, flea markets, you name it, we'd likely be there. All over New England, spring to late fall, sometimes doing gigs with snow falling. This, was what doing 'safari' was about, and when we went out, we went out looking for big game.

Working that hard at doing it, created all kinds of new problems, as strange as that might sound, people began coming to our stand, buying our food, casually mentioning, 'so you're the Chinese people I've heard about, huh... funny...you don't look...' So I guessed that the word was out and around about us. I made endless mental notes about stuff like this, like a psy-ops addition to our regular menu, isn't that how subliminal advertising works?

Everything matters and nothing matters at all, right? Not even that we weren't Chinese, it was, all good, right? The sky was the limit, right? Ride that wave all the way to the beach, right? Attendee's at these events would smell our food wafting on the air, and be told it was coming from, the 'Chinese people' so, virtually everyone expected us to be Chinese people. Even if an event was in the middle of the woods, or way out on the water, on a freaking boat-pier, it didn't matter; the Chinese people'd be there, rocking out as usual with their own crowd, their own power, water, supplies and gas for cooking, doing business with our own Oriental music blaring. Booking as independents, booking free-lance, as guerilla vendors, eliminated virtually all barriers for successful entrance into commerce.

We were totally mobile baby, and when the show closed; we just folded up the trailer, vanished, and headed off to the next event. It wasn't long before we began seeing the same people at different kinds of fringe events. Our reputation as the place to eat at festivals began becoming a talked about thing. Before long, our 'crowd' began finding us at shows, having sought us out, tracking us down by the smell of our cooking food. Learning to identify 'our crowd' became ridiculously obvious from then on. Actually, they were pretty obvious all along, but I was still learning. I felt I'd gone miles on the learning curve since beginning, and began getting comfortable with the 'anything could happen' aspect of it all. That enabled seeing the need for a 'presence', like the 'face' of the business, and an advertising strategy based on not only what we were all about, or weren't all about, but based upon what 'our crowds' likes and dislikes were all about, and how much they were willing to spend on getting what they wanted. If you give people what they want, they'll buy it. This is not rocket science. If you build it, they will come, if you cook it they will buy it and eat it. Unless it's completely disgusting.

In guerrilla vending, once we got the trailer to an event and set up, the game would definitely be on. We knew the 'game', because we were the game, clients were the unsuspecting constants. The game, was the time-frame window of opportunity the event provided as foot traffic. It opened when the show began, and closed entirely back up when the event ended. And so if anything was going to happen at all, it had better happen before that window of opportunity closed back up and vanished. Game on! Very often, there'd be very little, to no competition, sometimes, none at all. Usually because of an events location or obscurity. Because of these locations, like out in the woods or something, we had to be entirely self-contained and intrepid enough to go just about anywhere. And go everywhere we did, and everyone always seemed pretty glad we were there. We felt the same way. Whether in a field, in the woods, by a stream, behind a cow barn, way out on a boat pier, on the side of a hill, wherever people smelled the enticing aroma of our action, they began coming in crowds and droves to buy our food and refreshments. It could have been my brilliant repartee, but I believed it was really my cooking. They told us we were real, even knowing we weren't Chinese. We suspected they enjoyed the completely spontaneous theatre of experiencing us working through a Marriage Encounter episode while we cooked. We began recognizing and learning what advertising hooks worked best and integrated those techniques into our schtick. Guerilla vending is everything you can imagine about how low cost-no cost marketing works like that. You use what works best and forget the rest. But be leary of vendors that make what they're doing look easy, like anybody could do it, right? Real pros always make things look easier than they appear, because they've probably done the same thing over and over again ten thousand times. We employed every technique we could think of that might work, like I said, loud Oriental music on our cheesy little sound system, signs written in pseudo-oriental calligraphy, flashing red marquee lights, a temple shaped sandwich sign, but what worked best was the captivating fragrant aroma of ingredients cooking that brought clients following their noses. It was like an invisible sign that was everywhere, one that told you everything you needed to know, and then some. And the theatre of seeing and watching and smelling each order getting cooked, before your very eyes, smelling it, hearing it hiss and sizzle and letting your senses imagine how good it was going to taste, well, how good is that? Is that, better than any sign imaginable? This was the kind of sign that didn't have to be read, or explained, a sign that spoke all languages, one that explained everything itself, after that; the product actually sold its self. The most challenging aspect of the entire procedure; was learning to make every order look the same. That's, what was expected, the same, and good enough to eat, the rest of it was theatre for them, but like therapy for me.

I orchestrated the entire arrangement around five beautiful colors most appealing to the eye. Red, Orange, Green, Yellow, and Purple. The colors of the rainbow I was hoping to go over, the one Judy Garland was always singing about. Thickly sliced sections of sweet Red peppers, matchstick cut Carrots, brilliantly green Broccoli florets, chunks of Yellow summer squash, and medallions of deep red, Purple onions. It was pretty to look at, and convinced a lot of people into deciding on eating that before they ever tasted it. If you're anything like me, you might believe you are what you eat, you might even agree, that in regards to your mind and body, you are, also, what you think. Or are led to believe, and, therefore, let yourself choose to believe. So that ought to help in figuring out, what you believe, or, don't believe, and quite possibly even explain, why. If your cerebral nutrition is the intellectual equivalent of junk food, your ideas and conclusions are bound to be the equivalent of obese, moribund and layered with the fatty tissues of stupidity, laziness, and denial. The truth about anything is always well hidden in half- truths and outright lies. That's what sells products so effectively, that's what advertising's all about, seducing you, telling you anything that works, but; that wasn't us. We were about, giving you exactly what you saw somebody else getting, and made it look so tantalizing you just had to have it, end of subject. We sold untold volumes of food because some customers would approach the counter, seeing someone else's order and tell us, 'ooh, that looks good, I'll have that' based solely upon how it appeared. In this case, it was one of seeing, being believing. And that's, why the truth, is so often so hard to believe, because it either appears, or sounds, too unbelievable to be true at all. Does that strike you as crazy or what? For example, suppose you think there ought to be laws about some people wearing spandex outfits in public. Consider what their minds must look like, all trussed up, stretched out and misshapen, from being endlessly saturated with misinformation, disinformation, out right factual distortions and endless product advertising supposing to be about them, in their perceptions of themselves. That's, most likely what leads them think that way in the first place. This is why I don't watch T.V. and haven't for a long time, it hurts my intellect, like a toothache that interrupts my peace of mind. The mission statement for my desire to be the change I sought in the world; began with the up hill battle to eradicate nutritional stupidity. Stupidity being defined as the cumulative effects of television, television advertising, junk food, processed foods, the impact of high fructose corn syrups and cheap beer. We weren't in business to change any ones' mind about anything; we were in business to sell food and help people change their minds about their food options. And the primary way for going about that, was by letting their noses guide them to whatever smelled so good, then letting them feast with their eyes watching someone else's order being cooked, as it was ordered, and tasting it in their mind before it ever even got close to their mouths. Seeing in this case usually led to believing, like I say, and believing usually led to them having some of that Chinese stuff as well. Worked every time, no joke. Our menu board intentionally suggested, in really tiny print at the bottom, to not even think about inquiring about MSG use in our cooking. It simply stated in capitol letters, WE DON'T. People educated themselves when they struggled to read the question in the tiny print about what the answer to question was. It was a great Segway into sales dialogues. We were determined that if you were thinking about making a purchase, we'd be your best choice.

Uninhibited public relations like that, brought in sales, actually, lots of sales, and I found myself again, making endless mental notes about it, about not using something being key, that sometimes, less is more, that sometimes, without, is better. But the most incredible amount of our success; was based upon simply empowering clients to be, themselves, the changes they were seeking in their worlds, enabling them to be part of their own solutions based on the choices they were making about their lives, being no longer content to remain just, quasi-happy about still being part of their problems of powerless disappointment and dissatisfaction. Gandhi was in my heart, but still, I was reluctant to create change in the world wearing a diaper. I would've looked even sillier than not even being not Chinese. What I'm talking about instead, is building connections between people one plate of noodles at a time. People it seems, turn out to be a lot more attentive listeners when they're eating, being fed, being made happy. And generally speaking, a happy crowd; is quite possibly, a hungry crowd as well. So, if you're gonna dig for gold, you gotta know where to dig. Each and every order was cooked and prepared identically, with the same dedicated attention to color and detail and the simple love of doing it at all. Our counter was endlessly crowded with people eating and talking, or standing in front, waiting to order or being a part of the lingering conversations surrounding our presence. To us, it seemed they apparently understood what we weren't about at all, about schlepping corporate products, or shilling their over priced pseudo-foods, or sugary cola confections. And they, our clients weren't about buying them either, or even having them as a part of their lives. We made food for you, as you ordered it and then, let you watch it getting cooked, making you an entire part of the process. People loved it; it was like being on television. We were about defining, and playing our own game, and playing it to the max, as the 'alternative' option. And so that, is exactly what we did, and by this time, we were getting pretty good at it too. I would guess 'good' at this point, meant that getting rid of anywhere between two and three hundred pounds of noodles in seven or eight hours was average, sometimes more, but hardly ever, less. Believe me, it's a lot easier saying that, than doing it. For one thing, it was a lot noisier, and there were moments of all out vending chaos at some shows, where it'd be nothing but people waving money over the heads of people in front of them, at the counter, and just real chaos. It was no wonder Glenda developed her numbering system. It was like being in the zoo at feeding time, highly instructive, but something that gave you plenty to think about when it was over.

But we egged it on, we were just getting what we asked for, and how often does that ever happen? Understand, we didn't resist presenting ourselves as such. As the alternative, as the option, always set up a bit away from the other vendors, with our weird oriental music always playing in the background, making you feel you were part of a cultural film about China, made real by the heavenly cooking smells of toasted sesame, garlic and ginger, and the curious lingering crowds, eating and ordering, inhaling those robust, intoxicating fragrances. This; for example, is a thing you virtually never, ever, see at events, that of crowds of people lingering around French fry vendors, or fried dough people or sausage purveyors. It just isn't done; you make your purchase and go. In the business they're referred to as 'snatch' joints, you grab and go. People used purchase from us, and then hang out eating, and that, drew in even more people wondering what was going on 'over there'. We used this aggregation, as a source of advertising, knowing other event goers would be naturally curious about what was going on at the 'Chinese peoples' place. And so, we added that to the game and played it hard, for a long time. Twenty-five years. That game was about discovering exactly what people wanted, and then, giving them exactly that. It worked every time. Again, it wasn't exactly rocket science, but it was definitely a well-calculated win-win scenario, with very little genius involved in it at all. What's most important however, is that I believed we could make a difference, even if it was only a fraction of a fraction, in my mind it was still better than doing nothing at all. I believe the world would be a much different place if stupidity was painful, but it isn't, or ever has been, or likely ever will be, so, I was working to eradicate nutritional stupidity, because, I really cared. And I really did. I still do but now feel, more than ever before, that we're hopelessly outnumbered by people whose world, begins and ends at the tip of their noses. But if you're intending to work that hard for something so noble, there's got to be something that makes you feel satisfied with your results. And one of the most satisfying aspects of being a small businessperson; is being small enough to know many people by name and demonstrate by your efforts you really care about them. I depended upon making them as happy as I could because I needed them to come back, especially with other hungry people. Therefore, everybody got treated politely, everyone was important, and respect too, was part of what being who we were trying to be was all about. You'll rarely get treated as sincerely by sausage vendors or grease merchants of any kind, trust me, after you grab, you're expected to go because you'll just be in the way of the next sale. We were that serious about our vending strategies; which had already started becoming part of our work and too much investment to keep just continually breaking even. We were about treating our clients right and creating a welcoming narrative of programing so you'd tell others about us and come back again and again. And soon it began working better than I had ever hoped or expected it to and people began coming back time after time, event after event bringing hungry friends along with them. More accurate targeting and cultivating of our target market, enabled us to begin 'hitting' the bulls- eye more often than 'missing' it or just getting close. So, when people began finding us at events, it's because they were meant to find us because we represented something they believed in about themselves. They usually just followed their noses. We, were beginning to know who these people were, and where they'd most likely be found congregating if they were out there, anywhere, to spend some money and have a little bit of fun. We went on safari, searching them out like an exotic species. And it was while on safari, when something began becoming more noticeably curious. Again and again, we were experiencing a most unusual problem, event after event until it began seeming almost routine. We began seeming to never have enough stock and product on hand to accommodate our burgeoning market based sales. We seemed to be running out of food and be forced to close early at shows because of selling out. Great problem to have huh? We were excited about having done so smashingly well, yet mystified about why we were suddenly not having enough product to be selling to the very end of the event. Things never used to be like that. Either portioning was way off, which meant we were serving out too much for too little money, or we were becoming more popular and selling greater volumes than ever before, at every show. Somehow every show seemed to be demanding more and more of us. We began witnessing long, snaking, twisting lines of patrons dedicated to waiting to be served who were not going to opt out and grab a burger or some other kind of deep fried stuff instead. What they obviously wanted was some of that Chinese food they smelled cooking and were determined to wait their turn in line to get it. Some problem to have huh? Suddenly, that 'something' seemed to be continually limiting our profitability, like we were hitting an invisible barrier, one that wasn't obvious, and one that prohibited and limited our growth potential. None of this was lost on the other food vendors, while they had no lines of clients, we'd be almost out of control with business, and becoming a force to be reckoned with by holding our own. It took volumes of brainstorming before finally accepting the fact that the business had evolved to a point where it had to either grow and evolve, or remain the same and be content with that. Constantly, I was thinking about how the business could run, should run, and never, for even an instant, stopped to consider the consequences of the rock I was rolling up hill, ever losing momentum and begin rolling backwards, down hill, crushing the unfortunate ant, working so diligently at doing the business, and then, having the business finally doing him. Poor ant, a 'has been' without ever knowing it, before ever being a 'was', success it seemed had the potential for making him that has been, before ever being a, was, at all. But this ant knew there was no turning back, not now, not ever, there was only going forward into the future. Solving problems began becoming fun, puzzles of challenges to creative thinking, which as you surely know, is the mother of all innovative thinking. I had set the reality of the entire idea into motion, making it real by acknowledging it, and then, acting upon it. I had set out to move a mountain after all, and I began suspecting it had just begun budging in my favor. But the business, on its own, was starting to take off, starting to become like when Frankenstein, the monster, realizes his creator needed him more than he needed his creator. The business, and the whole schtick of not being Chinese, began taking on a life of it's own, requiring more of everything than it ever had before. Including more of me, I began feeling like I was just along for the joy ride and not in the drivers seat either. It was either grow with it, or don't grow at all. Success can be like that, a really heady experience, not only for monsters, but for ants as well. But getting back to becoming what you think, if you're still open to considering it. Consider that over time, not only do you become what you do, but, what you do, becomes you, beomes who you are. Like it or not, to a lot of people I had become the 'Chinese' guy. Look, everything you do is about what you believe, and sooner or later, everything you believe, becomes you. That's precisely how I got to be not Chinese in the first place, by actually being not Chinese, go figure. I'm imagining you've got a pretty good idea where I'm going with all this, I didn't think it was a crazy idea at all. I mean, I was making money at it, how real is that? As long as I handled volume sales, I could easily benefit from the hard work it required.

In a way, I wish it could've stayed as simple as it was in the beginning, but nothing ever stays the same forever. Not only that, but I should've realized at some point, it had to come to an end, had to have a finale of some kind. But in the beginning of everything, you never stop to considered an ending of any kind; besides, I was more exhilarated about soaring than crashing. In the beginning of anything, that soaring sense of success is often the cause for over looking things as simple and as important as landing. On the other hand, crashing can be pretty instructive as well, but a lot less fun. The unfortunate truth though is, once you get a moutanin moving, the only thing to do is to keep pushing and follow where it goes. I had a hard time believing I was becoming a fledgling business success and I liked how it made me feel about myself.

CHAPTER 4

'BECOMING AN ENTREPRENEUR'

The way advertising works is by insinuating ideas into your attention span without you even realizing your brain has been tampered with. There's a few ways to go about this, but basically it's all about sensory input, suggestions that summon you before you even know you knew you wanted something you didn't even know you wanted. Pretty cool huh? But the real secret to my success is the same as it's always been, lots and lots of hard work, and simple, clever effective marketing. But I wouldn't be telling you everything if I left out strange, star-crossed kinds of good luck and fate. I suppose what I'm trying to tell you, is, that you never know who's going to walk on stage next in dreamland, maybe that's what makes it's so exciting. This is what I'm thinking lying there, stretched out on the bank of some pastoral mountain stream in Spain, all these years later, waiting for Glenda with our picnic retreat celebration. Luxuriating there in the sun, pre-nirvana like, eyes closed, listening to the burbling babble of the stream, weightlessly floating through my thoughts, a million miles from anything, tormenting my peace continually with pulling scabs off the past. Eyes closed, hovering around erratically in my thoughts like a dragon fly buzzing all over the place, my mind like a high speed movie, careening from one recollection to another. Staring through the gelatinous marmalade of my eyelids like I was floating on a translucent sea. Remembering clearly, exactly how things got to the point they had. Things just kept growing and getting better and better by themselves, completely independent of me it seemed, like the business had taken on a life of it's own, and was dragging me along with it, like it or not, and there was no use even resisting. Some problem to have huh? After all, isn't that what I wanted? Wasn't being successful how I'd wanted to be? I was wondering if I'd gotten what I thought I'd wanted, only to find out I didn't want that at all. This is why I don't do drugs; I don't need anything making reality any weirder than it already is. Then, I distinctly recalled the reason for beginning to live the accelerated version of 'this is your life'. Like I said, you never know who's going to walk on stage into your life and change everything you thought you had in place. At least, it's something I never expected to happen until it did.

And as I've already told you, that day, for me, came when a strange old woman appeared in my life predicting the success that would usher me into high gear and keep me there. She told me I should expect strange and wonderful things to happen and suggested I work that, into the framework of my life. She told me that she; was one of those strange and wonderful things for me, and it turned out, she really was.

So the entire incident was leaving me noticeably struck because when things you can't explain or account for happen, they appear to defy the odds of things like that, happening at all.

Say, for example, if the odds are one hundred to one of something happening or not, this, was that one time, and it happening, meant that not only could it happen, but it does happen, and it just happened right then and there, like that opportunity had just been waiting for me to come along. Like experiencing lightening striking. When you experience things like lightening striking, you have a hard time explaining the phenomenon to yourself, all you have, is the wonder that it happened as you witnessed it, and it's curious that you find yourself afterwards, endlessly wondering about things you might not even be capable of explaining. As in why did that happen at all? That's what meeting that old woman was like, I saw her that once, and then briefly, a second time, and then never again. I'm telling you I'd never seen her before in my life, or before that day, and failed at the time to comprehend the significance of her star shooting across the galaxy and of all things, crossing paths with mine. That I'd never seen her before in my life is meant to establish the fact that her appearance was lightning striking. Randomly, I thought. She was the star that crossed paths with mine in deep space, she, was the activity, believe it or not, that altered my life forever. Perhaps, even made who whom I am today. She was the event that changed my life and ever since, I've expected strange and wonderful things to happen just like she told me they'd happen. And they have.

So, anyway, I'm lying there, eyes closed, sun on my face, floating around in my mind, recalling meeting her in the perspective of deep space, silent, vast, timeless. And in that vast, silent timelessness, two stars go shooting past, precariously crossing each other's paths, with just missed, almost terminal contact. But instead of colliding chaotically, altering each other's trajectory, irrevocably, for eternity, before continuing to shoot on, out into forever. She's out there; somewhere, I just know it.

Like I've most likely already mentioned, my vending career was beginning inauspiciously with me making every attempt to be all things to all people. Big mistake. You can only be yourself; everyone else is taken, so try to find joy in being who you are. But her; she was a signpost along those un-guard railed learning curves, suggesting wonder. Like I said, you never know who's going to walk on stage, or when, and usually never, why either. Sometimes, that only becomes clearer later in the game.

Anyway, the final day of this particular horse show was like a bad zombie movie that wasn't well attended. All I could think about was trying to somehow escape early and erase this fiasco as a bad memory. It was hot, really hot, even in the shade it was really hot. It was like all the warnings about climate change hot, all at once hot. And really dusty too, you'd find yourself walking around, breathing really fine dirt floating in the air. Everything was dusty, even the little bit of grass they had there, was dusty. The only people there having any fun and whoopin' it up, being active in all that heat and dust, were horse people, and they'd be there being active doing horse stuff, even is there was lava flowing through. Things were not going well that day in the vending world, because, people just don't like to eat when it's that hot; actually; things were going terribly.

CHAPTER 5

'EXPECT GOOD THINGS TO HAPPEN'

I t was so dead, and Glenda was so pregnant, it gave me more than enough time to begin worrying and wondering what I'd do if I quit vending and tried something new. We had a baby due in a couple of months and the pressure was really on, if you know what I mean, to make some income, incoming. But instead, I was wondering about how I'd explain starting something new, before finishing what I was already working on to Glenda. She really hated it when I did stuff like that, and in my mind I could hear her admonishing voice chiding, '…and then…you never finish anything'. I didn't want her to see me like that, wanted to think of myself as achieving and putting my life in order. The thought of her being right was really making my soul squirm and ache, like a spiritual toothache. I was tormenting myself with self-doubt, full of gnawing uncertainty that what I was doing; I was doing in a catch fire kind of way. Anyway…drifting deeper and deeper into thinking about failure, my lack of success seemed due to some kind of personal fault that was mine alone. As much as I didn't want to own that, and, just as I could no longer stand thinking about it, a life-changing event occurred that I still can't explain. As if from out of nowhere a voice began speaking to me from behind and I heard that voice asking 'this here your business Mr. Chinese guy?' I turned, coming face to face with an old woman standing right behind me, leaning hard one of those canes with the four feet for stability, shielding her eyes with her hand

and squinting at me in the bright sunlight. I never heard her approach, it was more like she just appeared. She was old and wrinkled and frail, swaying and wobbling around on her cane. 'My names Betty' she said 'well' I asked her 'can I help you with anything?' 'Not likely' she replied 'not in this heat, besides I'm not here for your help, thanks, I'm here to help you'. I stared at her peculiarly, without understanding, asking with sheepish doubtful surprise, 'You're here... to help me'? She ignored my question and said, 'You must be some pretty good business man Mr. Chinese guy. You're the only one doing any business. I been keeping an eye on you and you've got what nobody else here's got at all. 'Ha' I laughed, 'yeah, the worst vending spot possible, people don't even know I'm here; no one can even see my signs'. 'Signs' she clucked, 'you can smell that stuff you're cooking way over in the Grand Stands, that's better than any old sign you'd have to read. Besides, you couldn't read a sign from that far away anyway'. So, I thought to myself, she's been watching me huh? Seems someones always watching from somewhere. 'Yeah' she said, 'I been keepin' an eye on you' she confessed leaning forward towards me on her cane, 'I know about stuff like these shows, I been in the business over twenty-five years, and I know people too'. 'Oh yeah' I said rather flipantly, 'how's any of that my good luck'? 'Because I'm here t' help you see the future' she replied abruptly, 'you got to expect good things t' happen, an' then they will', I stood there looking at her. 'That's my trailer over there' she said motioning at a beautiful double drop axel professional vending trailer open on three sides, with red lights flashing on and off in digitized sequences chasing around her overhead marquis signs, and I looked, and saw her gesturing at the festively painted signs that said 'Pop-corn' in big letters that made them look like they were popping. 'That's what your signs should be sayin' too' she said, 'but I'm not selling popcorn' I replied trying to get her to buzz off. 'I meant making your presence known, if you had a trailer like mine you'd be in a better spot, but no ones buying anything today, too hot. Only one I see here doin' any business today at all is you

Mr. Chinese guy. What's that all about?' 'You can smell the food I'm cooking over all this dust?'

'Of course I can, and so can everyone here…'she replied. 'Probably' she said, breaking the spell of my stupefaction, 'the only thing people like better'n the smell of popcorn, is the smell of Chinese food, and that's a fact I believe, cause I know I certainly do, and, I know people. Trust me' she said leaning towards me again on her cane, 'I know 'bout stuff like this, I been in this business a long long time'.

'You plannin' on making this some kind of career for yourself or something?' she asked. I looked at her, pursing my lips, realizing I'd never thought of what I was doing as a career.

'Well what I'd tell you, friend, is, that if you're, plannin' on stayin' in the business, you're goin' t' need a little bit jazzier real estate than y' got workin' for you now if you get my meaning. You want folks t' take you serious at all, you gotta look more like what your in the business of doin', and your trailer looking like a bird house on wheels ain't gonna make that, happen. No offense, but if you're planin'on stayin' in this business any length of time, you're gonna need a bigger, fancier rig, like mine over there, plain and simple. That bit more real estate'll give you a much greater presence, if you get what I mean. It'll also give you more room for your supplies n, stuff, y' know? An' presence brings a lot more business than what you're getting right now, here under these bleachers. Who put you back here anyway? Somebody don't like you or something? Instantly I realized what the old girls game was and asked without surprise 'So I suppose all this means you want t' sell me your trailer huh? Only problem' I told her 'is that I'm not in a position to afford a big fancy rig like yours. I hope t' be in the future, but right now, just can't' feeling vindicated by my honesty. 'What I'm sayin' is, an increase in presence is what's gonna get you out from under the bleachers and up to the midway where you ought t' be if you're goin' t' make any money doin' what you're doin' with your Chinese food thing here. You're workin' too hard down here. A bigger rig's gonna give you not only more presence, but more of what we call 'pizzazz' in the business, an' that, always means more money. Instantly I began feeling annoyed by the old girls game. 'We're getting ready for a bundle of joy that's coming our way faster than anything'.

'Yeah' she replied in a kind of deflated refrain, 'money problems're what I figured on before comin' over t' talk t' you. Money seems t' always be a problem, but it shouldn't be should it? Truth is…what I'm proposin' makes it almost like you can't afford not to buy it. You just got t' learn to trust in people sometimes Mr. Chinese guy'.

'Yeah' I agreed readily, trying to get her to buzz off, like some bothersome insect, 'it shouldn't be, but it usually is, for a lot of people, like me, for instance'. Then she switched tactics, closing in on me like a determined barracuda. 'That's your wife I see, huh? With the long pretty braid, gonna be a mother soon huh? Well, there y' go' she said holding up her hand, sticking up her fingers counting, saying, 'one, you're gonna stay in the business, two, you're gonna be a family man and need to make more money, three, you're gonna need t' be in a spot where you can make that extra money, four, my trailer's perfect for you to grow into, and five, and most importantly, I'm gonna be dead sooner n' later, an you know that trailer over there ain't gonna be much use t' me then. So I'm tryin' t' benefit from it now, before I go, y'see. You'd actually be doin' me a big favor, helpin' me t' get rid of it. That's how I see it Mr. Chinese guy'. 'Look, I'm sorry to make your life more complicated' I told her apologizing, realizing the old girl had me hog-tied before I even knew I'd been roped in. 'It'd be nice' I said, 'but I just can't spend money I don't have'. Man, she was persistent.

'Well' she coddled, 'that's the reason why, when this show's over, I want you n' your wife there, to have my trailer over there' she said, pointing at it, again, by nodding and gesturing with her head. I looked at her like she was delusional, 'Lady' I remonstrated, 'I've never seen you before in my life, you come out of nowhere, and want to give me, a complete stranger, your trailer and all the stuff that's in it? Stuff like this just doesn't happen everyday y'know? 'That's right' she said, 'it doesn't, n' that's what makes it happenin' now, seem so much more like the right thing. It's why you always gotta be prepared for wonder to happen in your life, cause you never know when it's gonna happen, an' y' gotta be ready for it by expectin' it. But not exactly for free friend, we're gonna want a few thousand for it, but if you ain't got it, that's alright too, you can work the trailer t' get it, and then, pay us then. Its all pretty simple, simpler things're always the best. It's just about learnin' t' trust people; an' tryin' not t' let money get in the way of believing everythings good'. 'B'sides' she said, 'you look t' me t' be a pretty honest lookin' fella, just startin' out in the world as I'm finishin' up in it. An' you know what they say, y' can't take it with ya. But y' can leave it to help someone out, an'get em' started on their way, y'know? Y'gotta expect good things t' happen, Mr. Chinese guy, and then they will.' 'So' I asked her disingeniously 'you just picked me out at random, out of the universe and decided I was the key to your largess...?'

'Yeah, well, somethin' like that' she said, 'you look t' me pretty young and deserving, so, yeah, it was you. You're 'bout the youngest fella on the lot, the rest of us is all ol' geezers. B'sides, it's just too much work for a couple ol' geezers like us, my husband an' me, it ain't fun like it used t'be, not like it was in the ol' days'. It was a lot easier then, n' a lot friendlier too, an' we were both a lot younger then too'. 'Lady' I pleaded, 'Betty', I said, 'nothings like the old days, except what you remember about them'. 'That's truer than you'd think' she replied. 'I used t' be young like you, n' life was all a dream, 'bout makin' plans and doin' things. Gettin' old ain't much of a reward for livin' such a hard life. That trailer there's just stuff we gotta get rid of. We're movin' t' Florida. Anything left over this time a couple weeks from now, becomes what we all become eventually, a tag sale. We're just tryin' t' get rid a this stuff while we can still benefit from it'. She was creating rapid images of success in my mind that began flashing on and off high speed like the marquis lites flashing on her trailer. I started thinking about me using her trailer and all the future possibilities therein. In moments, she'd told me about her long, hard life without a single self-pitying word. She said as a young girl, she'd decided her faith would give her the strength to see living through to the end. And now, that end was closer than ever before, and there seemed just so many living strings that needed tyin' up, she needed my help. That's what she said, that I'd be helping her get those loose ends tied up nice and set right, if I took her trailer. That's what made me, a part of her journey and her, a part of mine, it seemed we both needed something from each other, but only she seemed to know about it. 'So' she blurted out, startling me, 'we got a deal Mr. Chinese guy or what?' Man, she was really putting me on the spot. I retreated to my only defense that I didn't have the money. 'Money's not the point' she scolded, 'either you want it or you don't, what is it? Y' can't go on much longer in your little trailer, looks more like a Punch n' Judy stand than a Chinese restaurant. Y' gotta become what people expect t' see, or they won't see ya at all. B'sides; you'll get better spots n' where your at right now'.

What could I say? Everything she said was right and true. She stepped forward; close enough for me to see how deeply wrinkled she was, holding out her shaky hand, looking to to seal the deal. Instantly, I was embarrassed by my trailer, it really was like a Punch n' Judy stand. 'Deal?' she questioned again, before I even remembered shaking her hand and sealing my fate. Man; being old had little to do with her forcefulness, she should of sold insurance or Amway Products or something. 'You got t'take advantage of opportunities when they come along in life' she said, 'they stop coming when you get older'. And saying that, she winked at me, and I saw how beautiful and playful her eyes were. She was like a devilish young girl being unwillingly held in an old woman's body. 'Y' ought t' read up on Job in your Bible' she said, 'or 'bout Paul's conversion on the road to Damascus'. 'I don't read my Bible that much' I told her. 'I just let the spirit move me as it will, and try to work with whatever it brings my way'. 'Well, amen to that brother' she said turning and beginning to walk away. 'See you next week with the trailer' was the last thing she said.

Her, landing me as a deal must have been dramatically undramatic; I didn't haggle, or bargain or even ask what her price was. Actually, I didn't even try guessing what 'a few thousand' meant; I figured I'd never see her again. But the old girl had closed the deal before I even knew it'd been sold and purchased. I stared at her as she walked away almost afraid to feel too good about my possible future prospects. I doubt this would've ever happened if I'd gone to work, everyday in a traditional way. 'Yeah,' I echoed back, 'see you next week' believing I'd never see her again in my life. Geeze, what a fruit-loop, I was laughing to myself as she left, yeah, right, something for nothing; that happens in America every day, right?

The following Tuesday morning, still sleeping off the lingering effect of the previous three days on safari, Betty showed up with her equally ancient husband, Roger. They must've gotten up at like four A.M. or something, but there they were, parking my new trailer out back, by the barn. I had no clue how she'd even figured out where I lived, but by the time I got outside they had the trailer unhitched and chocked up and I couldn't believe how good it looked sitting there. Look out future, I was thinking; here I come. She told me they were rushed to attend a bible study group they belonged to, getting revved up for Sundays I guessed, and couldn't linger with formalities. Formalities? Formalities to Betty, apparently meant no paper work other than her address in Florida, where to send money when it started coming in. She told me to work hard, be kind, send her money when I could, and believe in things greater than myself. Wished me luck, got back into her truck with Rodger driving, and was gone before I could process the whole interaction, leaving me staring at my future. And then, I never saw or heard from her again. Can you believe it? I was having difficulty believing it myself, things like this just don't normally happen.

I looked up at the sky, feeling like I could jump up that high, into the endless blue and land on a big puffy cloud. Days like this made everything else seem possible. The business; believe it or not, seemed to be coming to me, even I couldn't believe it. I felt I was catching an updraft and soaring finally in the right direction, up, up, and away. How naively unaware I was of the tormented pageantry life was about to bestow upon me because of that trailer. Lucky me huh? Otherwise things would've gone on being unbearably boring, right? And a movie about my life, at that point, would likely put viewers to sleep. Actually, that might be very marketable product for insomnia.

The business had been my creation, it started with an idea, an idea that caught on, and suddenly, the creation began taking on a life of it's own. Becoming it's own legend, becoming in fact, greater, than even the man, behind the myth behind the legend. That was me. It made me feel as if I were joy riding in a stolen car with fate and not even caring about the consequences; I was having too much fun. I was certain someone was setting me up for a scene in the movie of my life. I think Betty may have been hinting about stuff like that, you know? Learn to expect the unexpected and all that.

I was building a gathering, creating my own hard earned success. A bigger trailer meant bigger shows, better shows, better shows meant better income, everything began seeming possible. Clicking into place. Things getting better seemed to be fated by the stars. Or something. I was becoming a player in a game I hadn't yet mastered, a game that can also become that which begins playing you. But playing that game at all; is about learning how to talk to people. Business teaches that everything is about building enduring relationships so; I endured, and paid Betty off at the end of our next season. Using the trailer began the up lift of a life experience I wouldn't be able to judge until later on, when I got perhaps, as old as Betty. I was on the road, I was in the sky, I was everywhere I could possible imagine being, I was becoming what I was doing, and what I was doing was becoming me.

So what if I wasn't Chinese, everyone treated me as if I were, and accepted the fact that I wasn't, so why rock the boat? It was theatre, it was schtick, it was profitable, and everything began 'clicking' right into place. I figured I had to be doing something right. I was having a great time just living and being myself, isn't that what living supposed to be about?

The revised plan was now, to engage the trailer in as many events that occurred in six months, spring to fall, as seasonally possible. That was going to require doing a bit of anything and everything to keep all those balls in the air. I was doing a lot of everything any way, a little more of anything wasn't going to slow anything down, just make it more interesting. I was navigating on the learning curves, staying afloat on the ebbing and flowing of cash flow, coming in and going out, just like the tides. I was trying to get my sea legs at floating my own boat, as the deck pitched up and down in the turbulent seas of opportunity. Money was coming in and going out so fast, that although I thought I was making a profit, paying my bills and current accounts, I wasn't certain I wasn't doing any better than breaking even, and you already know how I feel about that. Breaking even is fine for beginners, but after too long it makes all businesses anemic. It's like working as hard as you can until you completely burn out, and then, that's what you are, burned out human. Working that hard at anything can be character building, but endlessly just breaking even has never been a sufficiently good reason for being in business at all.

CHAPTER 6

'OVERCOMING FUGAZI'

'THE OBJECT OF EDUCATION IS THAT A MAN MAY BENEFIT HIMSELF BY SERVING OTHERS.'

—ELBERT HUBBARD

'OVERCOMING FUGAZI'

MONEY

I was making it, and it felt unreal because I was making it by faking it. As I've already probably mentioned, I was making up everything as I went along. If a problem came up, I'd solve it. I'd never done anything like this before, working for myself, flying by the seat of my pants. Using my ideas as my road map. Is that 'bum magic' or what? I'd never been in business, but applied utmost diligence and thought to my well-considered plans, sketching out mentally, the answers to the problems I imagined I'd encounter doing what I was intending to go about doing. Who'd be my target audience? How much was I realistically capable of accomplishing on my own? How feasible was success at all? I was shooting in the dark with no experience to contrast my conclusions by, but; still made some amazing, astutely seasoned, profitable decisions. In fact though, I think I was just really lucky. Because my best luck came mostly, from learning that what I didn't know that I didn't know, was about to come to me, and forever, I'd be a better person for it.

Just like my experience with Betty selling me her trailer, you never know where messages from beyond are going to come into your life from; it's like psychic post office. Primarily because you never know who's going to tell you about what you don't know that you don't know. And there's a very simple reason for that. I think of it as: rule one. You might want to memorize it.

RULE # 1:
'YOU NEVER KNOW WHO YOU'RE TALKING TO'

At this point, I need to tell you about Angelo. He was a guy that taught me everything I thought I already knew about going about the business of going about the business, so to speak. Angelo. Angelo was a right-on guy, a stand up guy as they used to say. Him and his wife, 'Apple Carole' became dear friends from the very beginning like they were waiting for me to show up at the fair. But by now, they're both long gone and I've never again crossed paths with anyone even similar to Angelo. Both, gone forever, to that big event in the sky, but what Angelo taught me lived on. Angelo was a lot older than me and I knew he liked me right away because he told me as soon as I first met him, that if he didn't like me, he wouldn't have bothered even speaking to me. I like him right from the start because he told me that he'd never bullshit me until he got to know me better, then began mentoring me about how to go about being what I was trying to be all about, simply by being myself. Angelo had an opinion about everything and he wasn't inhibited about letting you know either. He was a crotchity old pain in the ass that I will always miss. 'Be who you are kiddo' he always said, 'who else was there to be'? He taught me how to be confident, and how to conduct myself with 'the respect' I expected from others. Especially, from others, by being respectful to them. 'It's all about the respect' he'd tell me, waving his disgustingly chewed up cigar butt dismisfully. 'Respect's the only thing you get more of when you give it, and if it don't come back…forget about it, too bad for you.' So Angelo never bullshitted anyone. He didn't have to; he'd tell you just the way things were whether you liked it or not; 'cause there was no reason for him to bullshit anyone' and I guessed you'd have to go by that. Or not believe him or something.

If you didn't like what he had to say, 'too bad for you', he'd tell you waving you off with an exasperated scoff and wave of his hand, as if you were some bothersome insect annoying him. He'd only tell you what was on his mind so he never made any attempt to explain or justify anything. He just told it the way it was, or, at least the way it appeared to be, according to him.

He didn't get around much anymore, he usually just sat and watched, puffing on his big cigars, and he didn't miss much. He taught me everything he felt I needed to know about the vending business and I've never forgotten him for a second. Or his wife; Carol, the apple lady at the fair; who even looked kind of like an apple, she would have been a Baldwin apple I think.

But about Angelo, what can you ever do or say about a guy like that? Take him, or leave him. Truth is, he knew everyone, and everybody always spoke well of him, and even the people he didn't know, knew Angelo, and I'm not at all certain about how that worked. Angelo was just a guy who never raised his voice, was always calmly respectful, and knew people who knew people who seemed to know about things, most importantly; about how to get things done. And so, because of Angelo, things got done. I felt like I had something to learn. According to him, he never lied, so he told me he felt O.K. about always telling the truth; if you didn't like what he had to say, you didn't like it. What were you going to do? Shoot him? The guy was fearless; nothing seemed to faze him. Maybe he thought that he was Superman or something, I don't know, I tried to never judge him. Maybe, because he'd been shot to pieces in the war, nothing any longer seemed to scare him. Angelo was a real live war hero that lived to talk about it, but he hardly ever did.

'Being there was enough for me' he'd say, 'I don't need to talk about it, what good would it do? What? There's more to be afraid about living than dying. All your troubles end when you're dead'. And though he seemed reasonably harmless, to me, he was living proof of doing whatever you needed to do to get through your life. He'd show you both of his legs if you didn't believe him. Actually, they weren't really legs, just metal pipes with socks and shoes on them. 'Iwo Jima' he told me, tapping on them and making a metal clinking sound, 'a machine gun I think', he said, like it didn't matter at all, then put his cigar back in his mouth and sit there silently puffing up little clouds of smoke like some kind of Buddah.

Angelo was a hero from way back. From the time when there used to be such a thing as respect. Now, he was just trying to make the best of whatever time he had left with Carol, never complaining, living with the choices he'd made and all the aches, pains, baggage and bad memories that go along with just growing older. But still; a real live war hero, hence the cane; and that deserved respect. To me, it suggested he'd committed to his beliefs in things much greater than himself at some earlier point in his lifes' time, and apparently had gone through with being true to himself. Where he found himself now, was just part of a much larger picture.

It really hurt for him to be on his legs for a long time he told me after I'd gotten to know him.

But long before that, one day I saw him sitting alone, late one afternoon, around dusk, at the dark end of the midway, all by himself. Alone, on a bench there, under a street lamp, like he was waiting for a bus to come along, through this really cheesy little carnival we were doing, which in fact, was really doing us. We still hadn't identified or targeted our crowd, which means our market promotion was way off and there were lots of people walking by making gopher like faces, showing buck teeth, saying: 'ah-so, and you- Chinaman?' and, 'chop-chop' and shit like that. On top of the endless insane amount of noise a carnival midway is normally, on top of 'c'mon in, c'mon in, twenty- five cents to play-twenty-five cents to win'.... amid bells ringing, people screaming on the roller coaster, buzzers buzzing, balloons popping, the deafening sounds of engines revving up to red line in the monster auto smash up in the back ground, I met Angelo. No wonder he was sitting down there; it was quiet, away from the maddening crowd. All this frenzied commotion was like; occupationally hazardous hazards. After a while it became disorienting.

There he was, sitting placidly on this lonely bench, smoking the juicy butt of a huge cigar, blowing huge puffs of smoke and spinning his cane like he didn't have a care in the world. He could've been made out of fiberglass; he sat there like the perfect statue of an old geezer on a bench waiting for a bus.

As far as I knew, he'd never seen me before, and I'd never seen him before either, when he suddenly turns to me as I'm walking towards him, takes the cigar butt out of his mouth, and yells, 'hey...Chinaman, Chinaman, c'mere... c'mere and sit for a minute...' 'Hey Chinaman?' I thought; he's got to be talking to me, so I walked over closer. No one had ever called me Chinaman before.

His voice sounded scratchy and gravely, like some Hollywood mafia don impression. I raised my eyebrows, looking at him above the frames of my Ray Bans, checking him out. He sat looking over the frame of his tri-focal glasses checking me out at the same time. I was eager to meet some 'old timers', some real vending elders who'd done the circuit, or had had the circuit do them, what it seemed to be doing to me right then. People everywhere always talk about the 'good old' days, so I've always been curious about what made them so freeking wonderful, so I took off my apron and drifted closer in his direction. I walked up to him, seeing instantly that he, too, was a food vendor at the fair; noticing he still had his cash apron on. His oily coiffed silvered hair was perfectly groomed, like he'd plastered it in place using an entire bottle of hair tonic on it. His tri-focal glasses made his steel grey eyes appear the size of golf balls.

His trailer, he made an immediate point of nonchalantly telling me; was situated on the corner of the mid way, exactly in the middle of where all the foot traffic was. He was referring to his business savvy, 'a place', he told me, delicately knocking the ash off of his cigar 'where I should be, not, way down where I was in the middle of nowhere. There wouldn't be any competition up there' he told me, 'because he was selling; of all things; salads', which I thought was pretty daring, considering that his age group probably weren't big salad types, and more likely, meat and potato's types from a different generation. 'You got to learn about where the real action is kiddo' he told me, 'and then, make sure you're in the middle of it, especially if you're planning on making any large in this racket as a vendor'. 'Large' was his reference to making a good profit.

He looked at me, sniffed, then tossed his head back, off to the left, kind of shrugging, acting as if he were entirely ambivalent about his advice. You either take it, or you don't; it didn't matter to him.

'I'm Angelo' he announced when I got closer, but he pronounced it, 'An- jello'. And then held his open hand out to me, like the Pope, or a Mafia don, welcoming an audience to kiss his ring. At the same time he was holding out his hand, he commanded me to 'sit' he said, motioning with his cigar to a place next to him on the bench. I wasn't certain I should feel so honored by his intimacy.

It was late afternoon with shadows growing longer everywhere. This, for me, was the time of fairs I liked best. At dusk, when all the lights began coming on, it just seemed, so happy, magical, like… if anything could happen, it would. I sat down on the bench next to him, and he immediately began telling me the straight dope about life on 'the circuit'. First though, he puffed on his soggy stogie a couple of times to revitalize its burning, smoldering ash. Up close, it smelled like old tires burning.

'Boy, you ain't had yourself a new asshole torn, till you hear what Brooklyn has to say about you…'he said, blowing smoke sideways from the rope he was burning. 'Personally, I wouldn't worry about it, but, that's just me, but like I said, personally, I don't trust 'im, never have'. I smiled, taking his hand, shaking it lightly, saying, 'you don't trust him? Have you known him long'? 'Long?' he gasped, 'oh, just for the last fifty years or so, why'? I asked him what Brooklyn had to say about me not having any idea who Brooklyn was, or caring, or why whatever he had to say should be meaningful to me at all. Angelo raised his eyebrows and tossed his head back, making his eyes large while looking at me like I was a giant bug, as if he simply didn't understand or care that I didn't seem to care. 'Because' he explained, 'while he, himself didn't care about anything Brooklyn had to say about anything', he reminded me that he was the oldest of the vendor elders, whatever that meant. 'Every man steers his own ship' he said passively, putting the cigar back in his mouth. He says, 'if you ain't kosher from the very beginning, before you even get going, you're finished… finished before you even begin… that's what he says Mr. Chinese guy. What'd ya think about that?' I had no idea what he was talking about, because I'd never heard of anything like kosher Chinese food. I got kind of nervous not having any idea who this character Brooklyn was. I began wondering if he had a food allergy or something I should know about. But, while pondering that, he said; 'you're the new people huh? The Chinese people that took over Micky and Quinn's old spot huh? Geeze, there goes the neighborhood. They were there in that spot over twenty years y' know…I was already here when they first got started in the business. I been here forever, I know everyone on the lot. I spotted you and your wife right away two days ago when you came on the lot, but hey, you two don't look too Chinese to me…'

'We're not' I told him, 'it's kind of a joke'. He flashed a startled look of disbelief at me, tilting his head back, raising his eyebrows again questioningly, grimacing kind of myopically cockeyed, like I was a giant invading amoeba or something and said, '…a joke? What kind a joke is that? Either you're Chinese or you're not. What gives with that?' 'We're not' I told him, tipping my head towards him, sideways and shrugging.

'Oh' he said, 'I hadn't noticed. Wait'll you hear what Brooklyn has to say about that too. He told me right away yesterday; first thing he says he noticed about you; was neither of you's was Chinese.

Said that's pretty weird, didn't know what to make of it. So, what gives with all that not being Chinese stuff Mr. Chinese guy?'

Then, without waiting for an answer, and without even looking at me, very non-chalantly summarily announced; 'we sold a ton of salad last night...no kidding, a ton, it's going to be a good show for us. Best one in a real long time, we needed it. Got rid of a whole crate of tomatoes too, we haven't seen a show like this for years, tomorrow; we're going to run out for sure. I just know it'. 'Run out?' I asked him, chuckling, 'run out of salad?' For some reason running out of salad seemed foolish to me. He looked at me as if I'd insulted his intelligence. 'Yeah' he told me, 'run out of salad...marone... what' y' fugazi? What gives with you Mr. Chinese guy? You don't see how this thing works?' I didn't know what he was referring to; I was a little confused about what he was talking about. So, I just sat there next to him, taking in his perspective of the fair. It was an exceptionally beautiful night, the sounds and smells created an air of enchantment. I figured him for one of the vending elders who might be able to help me see what I was looking for, which was learning about the business.

'Running out of salad, isn't that a good thing? I mean, doesn't that mean you've sold out? Isn't that a good thing, that you've sold all your product?' He looked at me with astonished disbelief, 'what... are you fugazi or something? Aye marone, you gotta be fugazi or something? Listen t' what I'm tellin' ya, maybe even learn something. Running out of anything at a show's a bad thing. A real bad thing, it means you didn't plan far enough ahead. It means cash flow absolutely stops, it means you don't make any more sales, it means lost cash. Cash that; could've been yours, cash that; should'a been yours with better planning, see? When that happens, the show's as good as over for you kiddo, at least until next year, better you should start cleaning and packing up. Better luck next time... Listen, you got to always know your market... you got to always know how much you can depend on selling to that market without ending up throwing anything away... aye, marone, poor planning, that's like throwing money away, Jesus, Mary and Joseph' he hissed dismissively, sounding exasperated by my ignorance.

I considered what he was saying; it seemed like a very religious thing for him to be saying about loosing money. I thought about it, making a mental note to myself about remembering it. Engraving it into my mind. It was an important lesson to learn; one to never forget, immediately deciding to remember it as: rule number two in the vendors catechism.

RULE # 2:
'RUNNING OUT = MONEY LOST'

It was the age-old problem of the five P's. Poor Planning, Produces Pitiful Profits. Other than that, everything seemed like it was going so, right. Angelo was making me a little nervous about being successful even though his information seemed valuable. I felt light headed; kind of giddy, thinking maybe it was all the noise, all day long. 'I didn't know Mickey, or Quinn' I told him confessionally as I sat down beside him, 'they just told me to park my trailer there; so I did. But there ain't much traffic down there, no one even knows I'm here'. Acting like he didn't even hear me, he said 'Well, they'll both be missed, Mickey n' Quinn' he assured me, 'they're gone now y'know? But I'll tell ya, nobody could do a hot dog like Mickey could. Man, that woman was really something', he said, nodding his head, looking off into space, obviously recollecting.

'I mean, she really knew her way around a hot dog, y' know what I mean? Mickey did, knew exactly how a hot dog ought be done right, especially one with sauerkraut'n stuff on it. Hell, that's probably why her and Quinn were married for so long' he told me, knocking the ash off of his cigar, apparently not realizing he was making a crude kind of joke. Or maybe he did, and was wondering if I'd realize it, you know, guys and hot dogs and women and all that. I thought about that for a moment, not certain if he was making a joke with a double meaning, or if it was my lascivious nature just to take it that way. Then he said, 'well, hey, maybe if they don't know you're here it's because you ain't advertising things in the right way, y'know what I mean? One thing you don't ever want to forget,' he cautioned, 'people always eat first with their eyes, their mouths second. If something looks good enough to them to eat, it probably is, you got to remember that... always. That's just the way it is, the product sells itself. That's what Mickey was all about. Marone, that's what my salads are all about, they sell themselves. They look good enough to eat; so they sell themselves'. I wasn't sure about the connection between those two, but asked him, 'Were they married a long time?' but not really caring. 'Oh yeah' he says incredulously. 'Since way before even my missus and me, and that's a long, long time. Since way before you were probably even born. Hell, I been on that corner spot up there now for, oh, twenty-five years, maybe longer, maybe thirty. I deserve it though, you know? And I don't mind for telling you why either'. 'I'm all ears' I told him, anxious to gain any insight a vending elder could reveal on the secrets of success. 'Because, I'm a pro that's why, y'know, you got to be a pro if you're going to make it in this business. And... you got to be proud about what you do too... proud to be what you're all about. Not only that, but you also got to love what you do...that's what's really important, that's a major key. Loving what you're all about. It means you like who you are and like what you're doing in your life.

Listen, making money is one thing in life, what you do to make it, is what really brings you joy. That' why I been doing this for so long, I really like it. Especially these little fairs, the lights, the smells, the sounds, it's all good to me, and...most importantly, I'm making money while having fun.' I sat there listening to him, what could I do? What could I say? I had no experience, I had anything and everything to gain, how could I go wrong? I looked at him, looked at his faded, washed-out striped short sleeved shirt from the fifties and his sun bleached, well-worn, straw fedora, with its' sweat stained brown cloth band around it. At his chunky tri-focal glasses that kept sliding down his nose, at his oily grey hair, and tried imagining myself in the future, after a lifetime of… this? Was… he, really me… in the future? I wondered about that, but it was a very sobering thought.

'…That you're wife I see with you' he asked, 'she's beautiful but she don't look too Chinese to me neither. Brooklyn says maybe she is 'cause she's got that long dark braided hair'. 'We're not' I told him again, 'neither of us are' I said playfully.

'Oh yeah, a joke huh…that right? He asked, looking at me sideways, smiling, 'like you told me; like a joke… right? Some kind of joke y'got there Mr. Chinese guy, whata y' fugazi or something? Look, kiddo, in this business, either y'know who y'are or y' don't, but y' knowin' who y' are's the best, 'cause y' can't be everything t' everyone, how's anyone gonna know what you're all about if you don't? See what I'm sayin? Not knowin' who you are n' what you're all about's fugazi see what I mean?'

'I been here all these years t' make some payola y' know not just for the fun of it. People here know all about me an' my salads' he told me, puffing on his slimy cigar, bringing it back to life. 'It didn't make me rich, but hey, salad's been a good life for the missus an' me. But I tell you what though, it just ain't as much fun as it used to be, like when Mickey and Quinn were alive, an' y'know, if you ain't having fun at what you're doing, you're probably doing the wrong thing.' 'Huh' I kind of grunted, 'Yeah, I guess so, I never gave it much thought before, (big lie) wow; you must really love what you're doing then, selling salads huh?'

'Hey, I been doing this for so long I don't even know anymore myself. When I got home from the war all shot up I thought my life was over. I was just glad t' be alive and didn't even know why. I did what everybody else did in those days. Stayed drunk for a couple of weeks, then got a job. Only what kind a job is there for a guy with no, y'know nothing to stand on? There wasn't no such thing as post-traumatic stress syndrome in those days. It wasn't till long after I got new legs I found out why I was always so depressed. I was broke, no legs, no future, marone, what kind of a story is that for a guy with big plans?'

I started out selling sweet potato fries y'know, to support the family, I pioneered it, y'know, sweet potato fries instead of regular potatoes, can y'believe it? Same thing as a regular fry but made outta sweet potatoes instead. Curley ones, people loved it. Y' woulda thought I invented something totally new! I thought, marone! People'll buy just about anything if you sell it right. I believed that vegetables and such were the future. You can do O.K. by 'em too, y'know, vegetables, if you know who your market is and sell to them. But y' gotta know who your market is. You try sellin' anything in the wrong market, it's goodnight nurse for you, know what I mean? But everybody loves salads', he went on instructionally, gesturing by rotating the hand holding his cigar in a circle like a little wheel turning, 'with fresh tomato and cucumber... marone. But above all, you got t' always be respectful to everybody, especially the other venders. Respect is one of the few things you get more of when you give it. But you don't ever tell anybody nothing about how it's going. You just keep on smiling like it was going great, even if it ain't and that, keeps them wondering. But above all, you got to always be polite and respectful.' Man, I thought, this guy's really making the most of his break period; giving me plenty to think about.

'And... you got to always be thinking about the future' he told me. I felt like I should have been taking notes.

'Life's about making choices' he said, being in business is no different; it's about making choices, solving problems and filling needs, just like anything else. An' remember always too, if something ain't worth doing; why bother doing it at all? If it ain't fun, don't do it, or stop doing it an' do something else. Anything worth accomplishing in life, is just like it is in business, its' got to be worked hard for, otherwise it don't mean a thing', he said matter of factly, sitting there, like a self-satisfied Buddah, considering the wisdom of what he'd just said, toking on his juicy smoldering rope, holding it like a delicacy between his fingers, ever so daintily. 'Yeah' I suppose I'd have to agree with you about that; working for my self's been a real adventure so far'. 'It should be…marone; these're the days of your life unfolding. In the war I was so Goddammed scared I was gonna get killed, but I didn't, an' afterwards all I had t' be scared about was earning a living, and boy, that wasn't easy. If it'd been easier; more people would've been doing it. But it made me work even harder.' 'How many people you see here sellin' Chinese food…huh?

Not everybody's cut out to be a hero y'know. Or sell Chinese food either, especially not even being Chinese, and you can take that to the bank.' 'I don't care about being a hero as much as I care about being a success, even just a minor success would be O.K. too I guess' and let my voice trail off, wondering how fatherhood was going to be. 'Oh yeah? Well let me tell you' he said, 'that from my experience, anything in life worth doing at all is worth doing right the first time and getting it done. If you're planning on working for yourself-you're gonna be working a lot harder for one thing, and for that, you got to get compensated somehow, for the time and trouble it takes. You'll actually be saving time, money and a whole lot of headaches by just knowing what your business is all about in the first place. You get to know what it's all about by knowing what it's not all about. By knowing what your keystone is.' 'But I don't know what a keystone is' I said innocently. He looked at me directly, through his trifocals, accompanied by a knowing, soured puckered smile that questioned me for even wondering about it. 'Man, you really got t' be fugazi or something…? Keystone? Huh? Maron…? What gives? A keystone, it's what holds bridges up, a keystone, it's how you know if you're making any money or not. Aye yi-yi…marone… a keystone y'know…a keystone is like your 'break-even' point, see, once you hit your keystone, it means you ain't loosin' money see?'

Angelo's advice struck me as very seasoned wisdom from the school of hard knocks, but try imagining my surprise at him so openly divulging his operating theories, practically acquired no doubt, to me? Why me? Why was he bothering to be so candid to me I wondered, he didn't even know me, or who I was. Or so, I thought. Up until then, no one in the vending profession seemed open to sharing or telling me anything at all about the business, operating on the premise that what I didn't know, was more profitable to them. It began becoming obvious when I'd ask questions about the business and the other vendors I'd asked; would answer, I don't know. How could they not know? And, because he was telling me the kind of advice, the kind of knowledge and encouragement I was searching for, hoping to hear, I was unprepared for it when it came, not even realizing it coming from the accumulated wisdom of a vending elders. Shrewd marketing wisdom isn't the kind of thing you learn in school, but its depth was immediately apparent to me. Translated that means: how do you go about making money doing this, in other words. There was momentarily silence between us; the sounds of the fair seemed far away, wistful, almost melancholy and sad. 'How's that spot down there treatin' ya?' he asked 'making any money?' looking at me slyly. I looked at him blankly.

'I know, I know', he said before I could answer anything, waving the hand holding his cigar several times, acting bothered, like he was shooing away mosquitoes. 'It's none of my business, but you gotta figure your keystone out right away, learn how to pace yourself, get a sense of what's possible. This show only goes on for so long you know, get what I mean? How t' set yourself up for a long weekend. Today's only Friday y'know, we got two more days to make things happen, after that... what's the point? This place is gonna be a ghost town.' And saying that, he held up the palm of his right hand, moving it up and down questioningly, like he was weighing something invisible. Like he was weighing the amount of money he expected to make between here and there. 'I'm not even sure what my keystone even is' I confessed, 'I guess I'm just hoping to make some money'. 'Hoping to make some money?' He moaned, 'marone, you are all fugazi! Jesus, Mary n' Joseph, y' don't come here hopin' t' make some money, y' come here intending t' make some money, intending to make as much money as you possibly can', and he looked at me; arching his eyebrows above his glasses with a look of dismay. 'A keystone...' he said, 'Remember? It's what holds up bridges and arches… you use it to hold up your business, to determine your profitability. Marone, what's your time worth? Are you selling enough product to make it worthwhile? Are you charging enough?

How do you know if you're set up in the right spot? Is it making you any money? You got any good traffic? Marone…what gives with you young guys today?' 'I think the whole world's gettin' fugazi.' I didn't know what to think, so I asked him, why he felt so comfortable telling me all this? Suddenly, dropping all pretenses, looking at me as if I should be pitied, like he was seeing himself in his own past he said, 'because you look like a good kid that needs a break and some straight dope about this business from someone who knows it, even if you ain't Chinese, so it may as well come from me…take it n' use it, or take it n'lose it, it's all the same t' me'. At that point, he agonizingly hoisted himself up using his cane as the legs he no longer had, bending and twisting as he rose, announcing, 'I gotta get back to my trailer' he said, stabilizing himself on his legs before beginning to crab- walk away. 'I been on break too long, we're getting' t the dinner hour and time, in this business, is money y'know? Besides, you'll do what you'll do with my advice; know what I'm saying? Boy-o-boy though, you better get your head on straight' he told me as he began walking away. 'You might surprise yourself and end up being successful, then what? But it ain't likely unless you smile more and begin acting like you really know what you're doing'. But before he got too far away, yelled back over his shoulder, 'that's Brooklyn set up right across from you…them games of chance, that's him, he's probably been keeping an eye on you, he keeps track of everybody'.

'Especially everybody else's' numbers and writes 'em down too, keepin' track of everyone, not just his own. Just make sure you're keeping track of your own numbers'. Then he walked away, leaving me alone on the bench. I watched him wobbling off into the distance, back into the on going chaotic flashing, gonging, buzzing, shouting sounds of the midway now in full tilt with colored lights flashing on and off everywhere. Everything about it reminded me of a few personal experiences from the early seventies, which also left me with plenty to think about afterwards.

I felt like I'd taken a crash course on economics, marketing, promotion and public relations all in about fifteen minutes, I actually felt a little overwhelmed. It seemed a lot to process all at once. Walking back to my trailer, made me realize what valuable information Angelo had shared with me, information he'd gathered, win or lose over the years of his life. I could hear all the action, but couldn't benefit from it. He was right about many things but mostly right about the fact that, if it were easier, more people would be doing it. It got me thinking about everything, all at once, again. Imagining and wondering what the story was going to be with Brooklyn who ever that was, and if I'd ever get beyond 'fugazi'.

CHAPTER 7

'THE BROOKLYN SCHOOL OF ACCOUNTING'

'Experience is the name everyone gives to their mistakes'

—Elbert Hubbard

Following the meandering path of seasonal work as a noodle merchant, led before too long, straight away into the curious world of Carnies' and carnivals as well as any other imaginable outside event I could think of, and manage to wangle my way into. I became almost as good a 'pitch' man as any midway barker. I thought of it as working somewhere, not having identified my market yet. Only then, was I becoming aware of my innate talent and love, for 'schmoozing'. Sometimes relying on the very necessity of it and doing it as convincingly as I could, to produce sales. I began thinking of 'schmoozing' as a viable marketing strategy, as live inter-active guerrilla theatre with random, unsuspecting guest appearances of complete strangers. Being at work began becoming fun too. I began looking forward to going to work, now how cool is that? People soberly began asking me if I really was Chinese (it was pretty obvious I wasn't...but hey; I could've been...) and I told them honestly, no. Like it wasn't already obvious enough I wasn't. That got a lot of confused looks I learned to use as a segway into marketing conversations with complete strangers. You simply wouldn't believe some of the things complete strangers will confide in you, especially if they don't know you, or they know that you don't know them either, so never forget… you never; ever, know who you're talking to.

But to make them feel more comfortable with their observations of me, and because I was trying to get them to buy food and because I was trying so hard to be successful, I'd smile and reassure them, that yes, I really was Chinese, I just didn't look too much like it and that seemed to put them at ease. Even though, it was pretty obvious I wasn't. I told people who asked that it was all done with mirrors and they twisted their heads giving me queer looks, saying… 'What?' I wondered if any of this was getting down on 'the big' tape? In most cases it was like being on my own sit-com.

However trying to identify my target market, necessitated I become comfortable talking to people, living the somewhat, vagabond lifestyle of 'on the road' with a family. I'd booked any show or event, anywhere, endlessly seeking my niche, attempting my best to operate profitably. On the other hand, living the life of being part of a traveling Gypsy world of professional carnival people enabled me to see and be, part of a world and a way of being very few outsiders ever become familiar with. It's perhaps, almost the perfect contradiction in terms, like saying Amish stand up comedy, or Latin graffiti, or something of that vain. Of this, I speak of the 'behind the scenes' carnival people, a rare breed indeed. They inhabit an alternate universe of people who make no pretense about not fitting into 'regular' society anywhere, because; they have no reason or desire to fit in anywhere, or to be any part at all, of any regular society…my kind of people. Way out there, living life on the very serrated edges of living life. At the closest cutting edge of living life at all. Highly privative, idiosyncratic, peculiarly secretive, curiously mysterious, tribal-like, living in trailers, and endlessly traveling, grinding out weird, long hours for cheesy money, and to many of these people, there's no such thing as homelessness. They embody the very living substance of survival skills in motion; like the people you see in the beginning of Mad Max movies.

Often having just enough money to get to the next set up. This carney kind of lifestyle offered a business management education no ordinary accredited institution of higher learning could ever begin to develop or implement. I had intensive on the job learning opportunities of the basics of how to spot a sucker; how to string 'em along. How to out fox the foxes. How to create false wins. How to talk it up big, actually; that, sounds frighteningly like what Hedge Fund managers do too. But either way; you're either born with it; raised up in it; or stumble on it like I did. Being arcane means it's difficult to learn, like becoming fluent enough in Swedish to do car repair from a manual. Including knowledge of all the magic words and phrases and incantations mechanics the world over know. I speak to you here, of my own prudent guidance and instruction from therein, the Brooklyn School of Economics.

From this, I am delighted to inform you, evolved the genesis of my own closely held theories of economy and accounting. Taught to me by as distinguished a professor as ever, who also happened, coincidently, to operate several 'games of chance' tent set-ups at the carnival, as well. It was from this labrythine arena of early instruction and erudition the fundamentals of what became ultimately, my finely tuned economic understandings of how things operate in parallel universes began.

Early lessons instructed that if there was any ONE thing that was truer than anything else in life; something that was truer than true, because it always has been and always will be, it can only be this nugget of knowledge. You might even ebrace it as Rule #1 which if you remember is:

YOU NEVER REALLY KNOW WHO YOU'RE TALKING TO.

It's, precisely because of this; of never really knowing to whom one may be speaking, whenever you may find yourself perorating, that the one thing that is NEVER, EVER, talked about, (at least according to the Brooklynn School of conomics...), is: JUICE. You might know Juice as Simolians. Bangers. Ching. Large. Denaro. Bread. Dough. Bucks, whatever you call it, it is; truly, the one and only thing that nobody ever wants to talks about. And for good reasons too. Because you have either way too little, or way too much, but anybody that knows what's what; never lets on either way, so anybody who does talk about it...who perhaps even, brags about it...ignore them. You already know what they're full of; they're just trying to impress people while spreading it around. Besides, what've you got to prove to anybody anyway? Prove it to yourself. It's about using your ideas to make a living, not bragging to everyone what a genius you are. And the less said in this respect, the better off you're going to be. And; that's about it; you simply never talk about 'numbers' with anyone, because even though everyone's got 'em, nobody in their right mind's ever going to talk about them. It's lack of etiquette. Mostly; because firstly; (Rule #3), you never know who you're talking to and secondly, nobody brags unless they're idiots or trying to impress everyone with their business savvy, or both. So that, being said, should tell you all you need to know about accounting and people talking about numbers. Besides... really...why bother...who really cares? You have nothing to prove to anyone except to yourself, and maybe to your wife, and hopefully not to her divorce lawyer or something. Thank God for that. Would a movie of your life be a comedy or a tragedy?

This is especially the rule, you might say, if it's about your own numbers. Outside of that; it's nobody else's business, or ever should be. Unless, like I say, it's your wife, but I think that'd possibly make her, an accessory after the fact, so it's probably better to just never say anything about anything at all, to anyone.

Even her. Ever. She probably already knows everything she needs to know anyway, women are extraordinarily perceptive that way.

The first time I met Brooklyn, I considered he might have been a figment of my imagination; he looked like a cartoon character. An old cartoon character; come to life, right out of the depression era Sunday funny papers. He embodied the comic character nobody understood, someone who grunted a lot, mumbling word balloons designed to keep anyone from knowing exactly what he was saying, or talking about. But...in real life; was as foxy as foxes ever get; sharp as a tack, eagle eyed, and as crisp as a freshly sharpened pencil point. Everything else about him; was theatrical affectation, perpetrated intentionally to throw you off the track of who you were dealing with, bumpkin or mastermind? Slovenly genius? Or arch criminal? He made me feel as if I was in a comic book with him. Maybe I was.

Early some Sunday morning, at a time when most people were either still asleep or still at Church, a time when normal sounds of silence made even the smallest of sounds seem large, when there was still fog on the empty fair grounds, making them appear as what they always were when the carnival was in town, silent empty fields with tents and rides in them, devoid of the crowds that would later swell. I was strolling around taking in the bucollic mystery of it all when I came upon an oddly dressed little man, standing virtually unseen, hiding himself in shadows where he could observe and yet not be observed himself. It struck me that he seemed to have intentionally secreted himself, partially hidden in the dark spaces between two ancient faded striped canvas tents, where he could become completely focused, making diligent notes in a small, leather ledger that he held in his hand like a hymnal. There he stood, innocuously hidden between those faded striped tents, gently weaving back and forth, only pausing momentarily, when he'd put his pen to his lips recollecting whatever it was he was so keenly intent upon recollecting. His shoulders were scrunched up entirely hiding his neck like he didn't have one, and so completely absorbed was he with his writing, glasses pinched high up the bridge of his squinting, wrinkled up nose, he appeared to be oblivious to all around him.

So completely occupied did he seem with his calculating and figuring, he seemed not to even sense me standing there watching him. Or so I thought. Intermittently he'd stop writing, and begin looking up, gazing blankly into the sky, making obivious mental caluclations, waving his pen around like a wand adding up those figures, performing invisible calculations made in the air, before furiously recording them in his book. I couldn't help notice how he'd frequently stop, and take a different colored pen from his pocket, before resuming his color-coded cryptic scribbling's. He seemed secretively consumed with encrypting his accounting calculations in his book. His attempted stealth made me even more curiously decided about getting to know him better. I wasn't aware for the lesson I was in for. Sometimes you get way more than you ever bargained for, this was that time for me. Lucky me huh?

Everything about him said 'carney elder' which meant, a colleague, an intriguer, a posessor of curious knowledge, and an obvious career vending elder with secrets I thought I could prie out of him.

His blotchy baldhead, accentuated by random shocks and confusions of delicate, wispy white hair, made him look like every image of a mad scientist. It was this; that provoked my curiosity beyond endurance. I began seeing him as an unlikely cartoon character and as I watched, he suddenly stopped writing, slowly raising his eyes up at me, above the rims of his dirty, wire framed glasses and begin staring silently back at me like a malevolent raccoon disturbed by sensing danger. He stood there momentarily, taking complete notice of me taking notice of him, then, sensing no threat went back to his secretive scribbling, paying no more attention to me as if I wasn't even there. He was old, ancient you might say, dressed in multiple layers of mis- matched, oily looking, respectable, yet, soiled threadbare clothing. Dressed as if he'd raided a used clothing collection box. Maybe he had. You never get used to what to expect when you're dealing with carnies.

Finally, he acknowledged my continued presence, by performing deliberately theatrical pantomimes of guarding the sanctimonious books' importance, snapping it closed and ceremoniously fingering it with perfunctory solemnity, replacing it into the inner pocket of his grimy brown sports jackets. He stood there, positioning himself with both thumbs under his clown like suspenders, putting the glare on me;

the eyeball, and began observing me observing him, giving me the obvious 'once over' from head to toe. I clearly sensed that me, watching him, made him paranoid because he didn't know why, but; I imagined him to be a clown with the carnival, seriously expecting him at any moment to whip out a horn or a giant rubber flower that squirted water. I was disarmed; I love clowns, especially sad ones or people who take the world, or, themselves, too seriously, the worst kind of unhappy clowns.

There's something elementally disarming about unhappy joyfulness. Do we ever live long enoug to be that unhappy? I hope not. He and I seemed the only people awake on the fair grounds that morning, and we stood there like statues watching each other, hearing only the moo-ing and baah-ing sounds coming from the 4-H barn. I decided to befriend him and began walking closer to say hello, pausing hesitantly at the perimeter of his fulsome odor and the effusive bad breathy smell of inexpensive strong alcohol. He stood there scratching his jowly face, pawing the stubble of fine white whiskers, several days worth of needing a shave. He seemed harmless enough, so I braved getting closer sticking out my hand to say hello, but couldn't help following his eyes down, looking at my hand, with chagrined perplexed displeasure, as if I were offering to hand him dog shit.

'I don't like touching people if I don't have to' he told me, 'it's bad enough my hands are touching peoples' juice all day' then he wiped both hands down the front of his outer jacket, like it was his own personal sanitizer. I grimaced slightly letting my hand fall slowly back to my side, 'beg your pardon?' I squeaked somewhat baffled. He just stood there, looking me up and down, head to toe, giving me his version of the once over. Then, clearing his voice and speaking in an overly dramatic tone said 'I can tell that you're a man that's willing to start at the very beginning of anything, before succeeding at anything at all'. He put his thumbs back under his clown suspenders, rolling his eyes at me behind his trifocals. 'You can see that in me, huh? I asked incredulously, standing closer, braving his reeking aroma. I noticed he was wearing a pajama top for a shirt, and his layers of clothing were stained, well worn and shiny, like they'd been ironed with used motor oil. 'I can tell' he said, interrupting my stare, waving and gesturing at me with a green pen, before replacing it into his plastic, shirt pocket pen saver sack, 'I can tell' he assured me, 'because I've been around for a long time, but more importantly, I can tell, because I know people. Maybe not always too well, but with you… I could tell right away, that you, are a man of the world, otherwise you wouldn't even bother being up this early… I know those roosters in the cow barn better than I know my own alarm clock, when they say it's time to get up, brother…it's time to get up'. 'You know that huh?'

'Yes,' he explained, 'as a matter of fact I do… thanks to the benefit of a pastoral youth…in other words, being raised up on a farm.' I could see he was wearing two jackets and the inner one had longer, protruding sleeves at his cuff. 'My young friend' he said, reminding me of an old movie, 'I have devoted my life to the fates' that living life today in America has become.

Not only that, but I make it my personal mission to know every lot the missus and I ever play, ever have played, or have ever called our home. We have no home as you may know it, the road is our home and it's been that way for so long, I know of no other life. And that is the way we like it, the way it is, the way it has been and hopefully always will be', he finished quickly. I was silently engrossed in considering what he'd said. 'Business' he continued unabashed, 'is what everything in the world is about, has always been about, or, ever will be about'.

'That; and of course, knowing what your business is at all. But in particular, is what anything and everything else in life is all about'.

He stood weaving slowly, shifting front to back like he was swaying from the motion of a ship, eyeing me suspiciously from way off like I was out of focus to him, pointing at me with his chin, aloof as if he were waiting for a reluctant reply from me. I could hear him wheezing as he breathed. I'd noticed that he'd said: 'anything and everything', a phrase causing me to wonder if he'd intended, with that jumble of words, to tell me that either: God was business, or… that business…

was God? It. was, after all Sunday morning. 'You're working here…with the fair… right?' I tried asking, discreetly, blandly inquiring, trying not to seem too personal. 'Work here?' he choked repeating the words, slightly turning his head, mulling over the phrase with consideration.

'My good man, I only work, as you say, where there is work to be done. But more importantly, only where there is something to be gained for the experience of doing so at all… otherwise, why bother? My advice to you is to learn to never play games you have no chance of winning at. I know because, as it just so happens, I own, and operate, these several games of chance and opportunity, which you see before you' he said, motioning and nodding with his head. You see' he continued; 'though appearances may be deceiving, I, myself, am the purveyor of that, which makes America, perhaps the greatest, among all nations on earth… That… which makes America a literal temple laden with prizes, and there; within that temple, providing the people of our great land, with the unlimited opportunity of achieving those sacred American dreams… and the possibility of attaining that ultimate fulfillment; which, by the way, is the greatest of all American experiences and desires bar none…that, which is: the random opportunity of gaining something for virtually nothing, simply by taking a chance at it. Not only is that's what right and great about America my friend, but this; all of this…' he said, freeing his hands from his suspenders and spreading his arms in bountiful notions of cornocopia, 'and… more…could be yours', he emphasized excitedly, breathing asthmatically, panting, 'could all become yours… by simply taking a chance' then spreading the fingers of both hands palms open, wide in front of me, let them slowly fall like the end trails of a fireworks display. 'This' he said again for effect '…is what America…is all about. What I'm getting at you might want to remember, and that is…never play games you can't win at, and I ought t' know because nobody ever wins playing my game'. Wow! The guy was wearing me out trying to follow what he was preaching about but I memorized his rule as,

RULE #3:
'NEVER PLAY GAMES YOU CAN'T WIN AT BY PLAYING.'

At that point though, I was certain, I could've sold containers of this guy by the pallet load! And I didn't even have a clue what he was talking about. But I wondered…wasn't he explaining the very fundamentals of gambling to me? I mean, even I know you've got to have faith if you're going to be a gambler but gambling to have faith? His peroration wore me out, like I'd been jogging in my mind or something, baffling me. I'd only known this character for about six minutes, didn't even know his name, or hardly understood anything he was going on about for about three or four of those six minutes, non-stop. Was he some kind of right wing John Birch type lunatic? I was pretty certain he wasn't carrying. But…you never really know; do you? Especially with carnies, you're never surprised at all. Try imagining Mr. Magoo with a gun threatening mayhem over his version of what's so great about America today. Political fringe nuts inhabit and live in their own versions of carnival abandon in America. As far as I could determine or translate, what he'd been saying, what he'd been hyperventilating about; was taking a chance on getting something in America for nothing. Interesting concept. Welcome to America; please to bend over. In fact, as I came to know, he ran a couple of 'pitch and throw' concessions where hardly anyone ever won, maybe never did, but…what I wondered; what did any of that have to do with America? Only then… did I fully realize he was telling me, that disbelief is an elemental component of the codified ideals forming the great American mythology of 'having it all'. Not just the notion of some of it; all of it. It's like being poisoned by 'gotta have'. Brooklynn seemed to know from years of cagey experience, the only thing sweeter than having your cake and eating it too, was having the chance of winning that cake rather than buying it, before you ever got to eat it. A surprising number of people really believe in disbelieving, because after all; you've got to believe in something, even if it's, Santa Claus or the Easter Bunny.

Disbelieving means always having something to reach for, or to hope for. It's why places like Disneyworld do such enormous business, because, it's all about the total suspension of disbelief. Goofy is not a real person any more that someone on the Supreme Court. People just really want to believe that what's true, isn't and what isn't true, really is.

Television makes great use of this knowledge. I've even heard that in the original Warren Commission report on Kennedy's death, he succumbed as the result of a hit and run motorist. But felt even Americans would never buy that story.

Believing something's possible, like people can, and often really do get something for nothing…keeps alive believing that it can, and really does happen. And if you truly believe that enough, may turn out to be true. Believing it might even happen to you; is what keeps you believing. Because; hey, it really could happen, y'know? Believing that you don't believe that you don't believe you believe is what 'it's' all about. Step right this way… you've only got to play to win…everybody's a winner. Now that's either incredible faith, or incredible stupidity. So let me confess now, that I truly believe; the world would be an entirely different place, if stupidity, were painful. We already live in a world where greed drives normally good people mad; making them do things they normally wouldn't do attempting to get all they can, while they can.

Often stealing or taking more than they could use, consume or spend in several life times. Marketing the chance of getting something for nothing was genius…what a concept. It's like naming your business 'Going out of Business' but never seeming to. I looked at Brooklyn and his tents and wondered what people who played and 'won' could win… an overstuffed cartoon character made in Mexico or Asia by underpaid workers in the lands of toy-topia? Free single payer health care? Unlimited catastrophic medical coverage? A higher bank savings rate? Lower food or heating costs? Five extra years of life in good health?

What, I wondered, could really be won by playing his all American game of opportunity and chance in the land of milk and honey?

The man was brilliant; the man had made a career out of selling the chance of getting something for nothing, a career of turning out silk purses from sows' ears. Worse, giving winners the pay-off of an over stuffed make believe character made by under paid, slave wage workers trying to achieve the same goal on the other side of the world. In America, as in probably any place in the world, will be found people willing to sell you a chance of something for nothing, a bridge, underwater real estate, it all depends on what you let yourself believe. More bizarre though, are the number of people willing to spend (gamble) money on the belief of taking that chance, on taking a chance by taking a chance. Is that faith I wondered? Can faith also mean gullibility? Like: 'this way to the exit'. I tried imagining, mentally calculating his inventory and operating costs of marketing 'nothing' and noticed him looking at me; squarely in the eye, with a distinctly Mephistophelian, mischievous twinkle in his eye, as if he'd been reading my mind all along, when he said: 'minimal overhead, unlimited potential' and took my breath away. I took another look at his tents, and to say they looked old didn't accurately enough describe them. To suggest they appeared well used wouldn't adequately convey whatever possible tangible asset value they may have still had. They were simply...shabby. What had once, no doubt, been vibrant, contrasting colored stripes, suggesting carnival like abandon, gaiety and chancy fun, now looked a lot like this guys clothes: worn, worn, and then, worn again. The guy looked the same way, worn as well as everything else. I noticed a knot of tape holding his glasses together as he pushed them up the bridge of his nose again, something he did about every fifteen seconds.

'You're the Chinese people huh' he said abruptly, 'new to the world... huh kiddo? Down there; on the outskirts of town...who sold you that spot? You looking to buy a bridge?

'The midway kiddo...that's where all the action is... the foot traffic... y'know...that's where the real juice is'.

'You could fall asleep down where you're located, tough break, that's no place for making any serious juice, know what I'm saying? Y'got to be up where the action is, cause when it gets dark around here, it gets darker down there, on the outskirts of Chinatown first. Turns into a real ghost town 'till closing, know what I'm saying? That's how I can tell you're an amateur; seems to me, you don't even know any better, how're you going to make any serious juice down there in Chinatown, in the dark? You know something about making juice I don't?' Now, I've always struggled with being patient about being critized but this was kind of condescending, and when he notice he was making me feel bad, launched into saying; '...that your wife I seen you down there with in Chinatown? If it was, boy; you'll be seeing a lot of me, if you know what I'm talking about, and I ain't talking about no egg rolls either brother', and he winked at me and smiled revealing a mouthful of crooked, tobacco stained brownish-yellow teeth.

Then, in sharp, sudden rebuke, sounding like a saw cutting through a metal ash can; came a voice from within one of the striped tents loudly declaring: 'I don't think so father, you're dropping anchor right here where you belong an' I can keep an eye on you, you wont be getting into any mischief … of any kind' And suddenly as if from nowhere, the front to one of his tents rolled up like an old fashioned pull down window shade. There, inside the tent, rolling up the front flap, tugging on a control rope like an old salt, was the female version of this guy, identically clad, except for her gigantic candy apple red Sally Jessie Raphael glasses that took up much of her face. On her head was a faded blue sailors cap holding her oily, bodiless locks that drooped lifelessly about her face, in bowl cut fashion.

At that moment, the guy sprang back to life like he had fresh batteries and said, 'you can call me Brooklyn. It's my name, where I'm from, where I've spent most of my life, what I'm all about and everything I ever hope to be about.'

'Well…I'm the new guy', I replied humbly, like I was John-boy Walton.

'Yeah, I know' he said, 'like I told you, I make it my business to know stuff, you're the Chinese people that took over Mickey and Quinn's old' spot, was that so clever? I mean to start with, you don't even look too Chinese to me, but… what's the point of taking over a spot that's in the middle of nowhere? Mickey and Quinn never made any real juice down there… at least none that I know of and I keep track of those kinds of numbers'

'Numbers?' I asked him, 'what kind of numbers…?'

'Oh don't pay any attention to him at all honey said the woman in the sailor hat pleasantly enough, 'he's shakier 'n a bag full of dead flies'.

'I'm Viv' she told me, 'Vivian, Brooklyn's wife; but you can call me Honey; Honey, everybody does y'know? Everybody does'…and she tied off the rope holding open the flap like she was cinching up a cow at a rodeo, like a pro, with a quick, double hitch knot.

She, also pushed her giant red glasses up her nose every ten seconds as well, and as she reached out to shake my hand, she noticed that I noticed how dirty her hand was, like it had news print ink all over it. Actually, she looked about as sketchy as her husband Brooklyn did. She noticed me noticing her hand, and not reaching out to shake it, 'oh, that's just dirt off them tent ropes honey, they're old' she cautioned 'just like us. He don't like to touch anything either'. The two of them I decided, were definitely either out of the funny pages, or from some other galaxy. I noticed how petite she was, like a little pixie, a gnome.

'We ain't got any kids' Honey said without being asked, '…it's just me and him, we ain't ever had any' she told me wistfully, clearly seeing in her mind vanishing scenes of what might have been, but now… would certainly never be. 'Nope, never had the time for that bit of heaven on earth mother' Brooklyn clarified almost defensively, taking out his ledger to record something that'd apparently just occurred to him, using a blue pen this time, not a green one. His wife cozied up behind him, looking wife like, over his shoulder to see what he was recording into the sacred little book. Reaching her boney limb over his stooped shoulder, Honey pointed a crooked, identifying finger at the ledger, chiding him, 'that 8 there, should be in green, not blue, and those two 7's ought to be in the center column, definitely in red, at least as far as I recall how things went'. 'Right you are mother, right you are, as always. I was merely attempting to fluff things up for a rainy day you might say', and he immediately switched colored pens and began his notation, in red this time not blue. '...But there's never really... any time that's the right time for that kind of thing then...is there my dear?' he asked gently.

To distract his wife's prying curiosity; he snapped the ledger quickly shut making it sound like a muted leg trap clamping down on a leg as he closed it, pointing the book at me, shaking it. His icy blue eyes twinkled with mischievous deviltry under abundantly chaotic, unruly eyebrows, eyes that were magnified by his smudgy, taped up glasses. His wife, who'd been standing on tip toes behind him, lowered herself and stood by his side, putting her arm around him, almost simian like, kind of swooning like she was still eighteen. Her and...Brooklyn I thought, wow, they made me feel like I'd taken too much acid, and I was completely straight.

She was wearing low cut red canvas sneakers with dirty white laces. I was close enough to hear the methodic wheezing as they breathed, like two old leaky pipe organ pumps. Honey exuded a similar fragrant body musk odor and smelled like she'd been drinking the same stuff Brooklyn had the night before. 'We been playing on the road probably since right after the depression' Honey told me 'when there wasn't anything going on anywhere anyhow; juicing just enough t' get to the next place in life...drifting. But Brooklyn' she told me, 'he's a genius when it comes to making numbers work, he's the one that got us t' where we are today.' 'Nah, age doesn't matter mother; only thing that matters anymore in America today is numbers. Numbers are what everything's about.'

'I thought business was what everything was about?'. He looked at me slyly. 'Business is nothing but numbers, it's like another language to explain things'. 'I know my numbers for this show for the last five or six years, got it all recorded right here in the Bible.'

'That's your Bible?' I asked him.

'You better believe it kiddo, think of it like the new testament; Numbers' he said, 'comes right after Deuteronomy, or right before it I forget, but it's in there, look it up'. Brooklyn held his hand up next to his mouth confidentially telling me 'I taught her everything she knows about numbers, and now, she never forgets anything, never been the same woman ever since, there's no longer hiding anything from her'.

'You shouldn't be trying to hide anything from your wife anyway you old goat' Honey's voice said. She looked at me, 'you should always know your numbers honey, you don't know 'em, you don't know your butt from a bucket. Knowing your numbers helps you to know yourself too, you got to keep track of your numbers, time passes quick, one day you're going to be old, just like us. Then what? You either keep workin' hard, or harder later, when you get older like us.' 'Well I'm still not clear on this numbers thing; where do they come from?' I asked innocently.

Come from?' Brooklyn choked, putting his hand theatrically over his heart like he was on the verge of a stroke.

'Knowing numbers is about knowing everything you're pretending to be in life' Honey told me, numbers is all about money, not just about counting it'. Saying that, she withdrew from the layers and folds of her clothing a wad of bills as big as a soft ball, and proceeded to expertly divide it in half, putting half in her apron, and handing the rest to Brooklyn. I noticed the bills were all perfectly collated, all facing the same direction, not some randomly aggregated Michigan bank roll in a disorganized bundle of wadded up paper cash. The two of them gave me the impression that I'd been treading water in the shark tank. They were 'vending elders', holders of the arcane secrets and knowledge of how to go about generating cash. In essessense, they had secrets to teach and astuteness about business basics, cloaked in a learned canniness that had the potential for positive aspects of monetary outcomes. They seemed as harmless as a pair of aged criminal hamsters on the forever treadmill of an endless lam, but I believed them, they had nothing to gain by lying to me.

'Not only that' Brooklyn said cryptically, both hands hooked behind his clown suspenders, 'Rule #2 in business' he told me, holding up two fingers, 'don't never trust no one ever…at all, especially if you know 'em.'

'Yeah, remember that one real good' chimed in Honey. 'Rule #3' Brooklyn says; pointing up three fingers and shaking them to an abrupt stop, 'never… ever, under any circumstances… talk to anyone, ever, about numbers, especially your numbers. Any one who needs to hear it ain't going to believe you, an' anybody that don't need to hear it, just don't need to hear it.' 'That's right' Honey agreed, 'impress yourself with your own numbers, you ain't got to do it for anyone else…but yourself.'

'And the reason for such discretion; is because you never really know who you're talking to, do you? Could be almost anybody'. 'That's right' said Honey, 'they could be tax guys or some other kind of nice people that want to help you…'

'Nobody ever needs to know you're business, better'n you know your own business' Brooklyn said. 'Yeah' Honey added, 'except maybe your pretty wife, but neither you guys look very Chinese…what gives on that?'

'It's the reason I chose Chinese food in the first place' I told her, 'because neither of us is actually Chinese'.

'You're going t' go far kiddo, with thinking like that, very clever, thinking like that makes your future looks very interesting. Selling Chinese because you're not Chinese, that's good… clever, but weird'.

'My good woman here and I've been playing 'lots' with our money machine here seems like forever… We're the only ones' that know our numbers, and, the only ones' who ever should know 'em, end of subject.' Then he shook his book at me verifying its' truthfulness. 'How're you going to tell if you're making any money or not? If you're that successful why would you want to tell anyone? Why spoil the chances of keeping a good thing going? It's like working in a secret gold mine, you ain't got to tell anybody else, if anything you got to keep 'em from finding out about it, Listen kiddo, talk is cheap, numbers is real, only numbers tell the story about anything'.

'So what's with all the colored pens?'

'The colors' he intimated, 'I'm the only one who knows what the colors mean, they remind me that the number one rule in this business is to keep your mouth shut unless you're eating'.

'All the time' Honey chimed in, 'just keep smiling unless, like he says, you're eating.' 'If you're going t' be in this business' Brooklyn said, 'be a pro, after a while you'll learn t' tell who's real and who ain't. Pro's don't need t' talk about it, they just do what needs doin', do it, an' then go home. But you got t' know if doin' it at all is worth your while.'

'If you're going t' work long and hard at a business, you got t' be sure you're selling the right thing t' the right crowd or brother, you ain't selling nothing at all' he said.

'Our play sells the best product that can be sold, a product that virtually sells itself, the chance at the American dream, the chance to feel good about yourself; it never gets old and has a great shelf life, what's better than feeling good about yourself?

'Making money doing something you like?' I asked him.

Honey looked at me, grimacing 'Mr. Chinese guy, you want to impress anybody, impress yourself first, you'll be a lot happier if you do. Life's about being happy being who you are, or in your case, who you aren't. Just be happy; everything 'll work out somehow, it always does.' And that was that. I saw them a few times more at events here and there, and then, they just kind of vanished.

It wasn't long after that things went downhill pretty fast for Brooklyn. I learned through the concession grape vine that one of Brooklynn's declared desires had finally come true, and he was on his way to heaven before he ever hit the surface of the mid-way playing 'some lot' in Rhode Island. Exactly the way he told me he wanted to go out, boom, one moment at the carnival, the next, heaven. I heard Honey tried struggling on with the tents solo until she too succumbed to not knowing or caring about when to say when. I heard the day she died of a stroke, she fell, accidently knocking over a stack of wooden milk bottles people had been trying to knock down with three pitches for over twenty years.

It was the first time they were ever knocked down completely, she was a winner and she never even knew it. I'm not saying Honey and Brooklyn rigged their games; they just made it more challenging to win at winning. Hedging their own bets privately at the same time, very similar to the way things are in the world today. There ain't much that's free, or easy in life; so, if anything appears that seems like it is; watch out. This is how my life's been. Strange things just seem to happen, somehow, always at the right time, the universe seems to click and people like Brooklyn and Honey or Betty and Rodger seem to come out of nowhere, and they always seem to find me. My friend calls me a nerd magnet, 'don't worry' she says; 'if they're out there they'll find you'. And I'm still wondering not only how; but why?

CHAPTER 8

'LEARNING WHAT LOVE CAN BE'

"NO ONE WHO LOVES MISUNDERSTANDS"

—Elbert Hubbard

The seasonality of outdoor events severely limited the number of booking dates possible, making it obsessively important for having the trailer booked into place ahead of time for any live action. The phrase: 'hey…you guys open yet?' became music to my ears, the very sound of income incoming. But that didn't just happen; it took lots of work getting to that point. Lots of figuring things out, lots of learning from the curve… Whatever the show was; invariably didn't matter; I rarely saw it or heard it. That was often a blessing, but also wasn't the reason for me being there.

What mattered, and mattered the most, was being in the right place at the right time when the event got going. Being where we needed to be and doing what needed getting done to make everything seem to have a positive outcome. Using everything we learned from experience and coincidence, and profiting by it you might say. There were enormous tasks involved in getting everything ready for an event, all the preparations, everything, from rice wine vinegar to trailer tire pressure and making sure the turn signals worked properly. I came to think of doing all this advanced preparation as: 'winding the machine'. Believing that a machine properly wound, would, upon unwinding, make what appeared to be impossible, look easy, as if anybody could do it. That; is the real secret of being a pro. That; is also the real secret of 'everything', is it not? Now; I've always considered that the secret of 'everything', seemed to be in finding a way of having ones' cake and eating it too, knowing all along in my heart, that the truth of 'everything' is about being prepared for 'anything' and not much about eating cake at all. But notice, there's those words again, 'anything and everything' and you might recall how I already feel about those words. Learning by doing, searching for that cake you're planning to enjoy eating, can leave you with scars that never let you forget. Yet, winning or losing, you either learn from every lesson, or continue repeating them until you do, getting all banged up physically and mentally in the process. Maybe even developing a bad attitude along the way, which is as self-defeating as self-doubt.

I was the face of the business though; so I couldn't let myself get too scared up learning how to become a success. Which is strange because, client and cook obviously saw each other quite differently. From my perspective, in the noodle kitchen, aproned up and feeling like Commander Kirk on the bridge of the Enterprise, people arriving at the counters appeared to me not only as clients, but as live inter-active television, creating continual live impromptu opportunities to act upon. To them, I was just some Chinese guy claiming to not be Chinese at all and yet operating a Szechuan take out. Go figure.

When it wasn't too busy, it was very much like theatre of the absurd, a place where 'anything and everything' was possible. Like, Movable Feast. Like having instant playmates. That really appealed to me for obvious reasons. But, if 'anything' could occur, and it often did, it was most likely to occur, right there, at the noodle counter. Especially on singles day, which often occurred spontaneously whenever Glenda wasn't around, but just as a sales gimmick though. However; you might consider that there are two very exceptional rules here about life. One is to never take yourself too seriously, and the other, is to never think you've heard it all. And probably, that you should never feel too comfortable with everything you think you know about life, living and love.

Especially, until the day someone comes along and tells you an entirely new story about a very old bottle of wine, a tale about 'everything' you thought you already knew. This is why so many people hung out, lingering at the noodle counter eating, not solely because the cook was a brilliant raconteur while he cooked, not only because the food was good; but the entertainment was even better. It was like being part in an ongoing psychodrama about 'anything and everything'. A crowd hanging out was better than any sign I could've ever had, regardless of how big or how many flashing lights it had on it. People began finding us wherever we were at shows and events, tucked away in little places, obscured by our location. They just began following their noses, looking for wherever crowds seemed to be hanging out, and they'd find us, the Chinese people. We began finding ourselves welcoming back old friends we hadn't seen since the same time last year. It was weird; it was like living in "Brigadoon". Virtually everyone we knew was from someplace else and we wouldn't be seeing them again for another year.

In concession work, you generally never see people hanging out at French fry stands, or sausage joints, or fried dough joints, but our crowds made other vendors endlessly wonder what was going over at the Chinese guys. And eventually, they'd become our customers as well, then they'd know what was going on. We were.

It was at an Art Show in Connecticut that 'anything' happened again. Early one morning, before even being open for business, coffee for myself still brewing (I sold coffee as 'Asian coffee' because no one had ever heard of a Chinese place that sold coffee) what I thought I knew about love gained a valuable experience.

A sonorously melodic voice congenially summoned me from behind, accompanied by three clear distinct taps upon the counter. 'I say' said this sonorous voice, 'is this establishment prepared for services I'd like to inquire?'

It took a moment for me to translate what was being asked, 'open?' I questioned, turning to face the counter. 'That is correct' said the voice, 'is this establishment prepared for service at this early hour? The voice belonged to one of the largest human beings I'd ever seen up to that point in my life. An abnormally large man, attired in what appeared to be exceptionally well- tailored casual clothing, but so large, he had to lean in on the counter to accommodate himself under my awnings. For a moment I was amazed by his size. The gold ring he wore would have fit around…you know…it was a huge ring. 'I say' his soft voice told me, I can smell the most delightful aroma of house grind and I simply must avail myself of it before much longer'.

'You're not from around here are ya fella?' I asked him. 'Indeed perceptive of you my good friend' he said pleasantly, 'and how, exactly, did you come to deduce this if I may so inquire?' 'Well' I began, 'not many people around here speak as if they were out of a Dickens novel'. This was weird; this guy was enormous; I couldn't take my eyes off of him. He was extremely well groomed, exceptionally handsome, with soft wavy, well-trimmed grey hair and absolutely gigantic limbs that tapered down to his hands; elegant and looking groomed. Calmly he spoke again, 'a cup of your choicest grind would be the better part of beginning my day' he said.

'You want a cup of coffee?' I asked lamely, not wanting to touch money or anything else while I prepped, but I served him a cup of fresh hot coffee.

'Here you go' I told him, placing the cup on the counter before him, 'this ought to help you along in the day, I'm not yet really open, and don't have any change; so, take the coffee, enjoy it. It's free, my compliments, come back when you get hungry.' This is what I told everyone I gave free this or that to. Like programing them for later.

'My good man' he said sipping his coffee, 'the compliment is to you and your hospitality. You see, I've only just this morning arrived here from Italy, and fear I'm entirely unprepared for America as of yet, all I have are hundred lire notes for your payment'.

I could hear myself laughing out loud in my mind saying, Italy huh? Right…hundred lire notes huh…right. I knew the airport was a distance away from where we were, but this guy; just seemed to turn up, out of nowhere. I'd run into my share of lunatics, dead beats and flimflams and thought I'd heard just about 'everything', but this guy didn't fit any of the norms, he seemed unusually creative and highly entertaining.

He could, on the other hand, I imagined, be a complete mental patient who somehow strayed from some group home or some such similar local restraint facility.

'Look' I told him, 'it's only a cup of coffee, enjoy it, it's free, welcome to America'. He looked at me brightly, smiling, grateful. 'I trust that you have sugar at your disposal as well?' This guy was too much. After stirring in an abnormal amount of sugar and sipping and tasting the libation, he sat it on the counter, then, displayed the contents of his wallet as if to prove his truthfulness. When he spread open his billfold, I couldn't help notice it really was loaded with wads of hundred lire notes, obvious because of their colorfulness that it was foreign currency, just as he'd told me. There was silence; it was just me and him. 'I'm a surgeon' he said sipping his coffee, 'a medical cut and sew man if you will'.

'I've only just this morning de-jetted from not terribly far away at your local international airport and haven't as of yet adjusted to your time zone'. Meanwhile, I was staring at him trying to size him up, trying to remember if there was a mental hospital nearby or something like that, an institution for the criminally insane he could have walked away from. But he was so well dressed, and he had all that Italian money, I didn't know what to think. So I stood there, looking at him, trying to imagine him as a surgeon handling delicate instruments with such massive paws and somehow just couldn't make it believable in my own mind. 'So you're a surgeon huh? In Italy right?' I asked him in lightly veiled sarcastic disbelief, believing him really to be some kind of total nut case, a real whack job that'd managed somehow to disappear from somewhere.

'That is correct my friend, a practicing surgeon in Italy for over twenty-five years' he told me, opening his wallet again and producing a laminated photo I.D. identifying him as Doctor Leonard Ekkertman, saying that what he was showing me was his Italian license for operating as licensed physician. I was confused. Then, he showed me his Italian drivers license as well, turning his head to give me his best profile. Meanwhile, I was thinking about my friend who'd told me I was a nerd magnet. She'd warned me about this; 'don't worry' she said, 'they'll' always somehow find you, and I wondered not only how, as I looked at this guy, but why? Why me?

Seriously, after listening for years about the 'tiny people' and the 'come on in everyone's a winner, come on in…' I just couldn't relinquish my disbelief in what was going on. I decided I had to get rid of this guy, had to drive this…lunatic (?) away by using direct invasive frankness. It's like when you fire up a welder's torch, when you hear that thing, click, and it breathes spark into life blowing flame, you know, you mean business.

It'd become been my experience over time, that nothing clams people up faster than a couple of well chosen overly personal type questions. Just short of asking the guy for example, if he was a child molester or something as equally nefarious.

I felt I just had to get rid of this guy; who seemed like he was never about to leave on his own; I had other work to do and didn't want any hundred lire notes or any of his other idiosyncratic craziness either. I had nothing to gain and nothing to loose. So I asked him; 'So, you've been in Italy all these years, what brings you all of a sudden, back, here, on such a beautiful morning?'

'My dear Sir' he replied in a soothingly robust, grandiloquent manner, almost as if he were embarrassed to even mention it, 'America is my original home, born and bred if you will, as in; 'the Chicago Ekkertsman's' of course'. My approach wasn't working the way it was supposed to; I realized I'd have to get more personal, go right for the jugular.

'But why, today, of all days do you find yourself coming back after twenty- five years? I mean…what do you expect to find? What's here for you to come back to, except maybe memories?' I was certain I had him on that one, and could expect him momentarily to take his free coffee and scram. Instead of scramming as I had expected, he calmly finished his sip, slowly lowered his cup to the counter, paused momentarily, and said softly; 'It's my home, and today, of all days, as you say, is to be the day my one and only daughter is to be wed' 'Wow' I thought, 'this guy is non-stop'. I had pretty much concluded he was an escapee from some asylum, but to humor him and keep him docile, I asked, 'Married huh? Today? You're going to a wedding, dressed like this?' He sipped more from his coffee, then; delicately placed it on the counter; the cup looked tiny in his large hand. He cast his gaze down at the counter, then; raised his eyes to mine, looking directly at me, directly into my eyes, like our souls were about to meet and said; 'I wasn't invited'.

'You weren't invited to your own daughters wedding?' I asked feeling his humiliation.

'I wasn't invited' he repeated, 'but found out about it and decided to go anyway, she's my only daughter after all, and so, voila, here I am. The concierge of my hotel is preparing my tuxedo'. I couldn't believe it, one of us, I was sure, seemed to be having a psychotic episode, and now, I wasn't sure which of us it was. He sipped again at his coffee, freely explaining the dimensions of his insanity.

'You see' he said, 'I've actually held myself in exile in Europe these last twenty-five years. Working as a surgeon, living well, true, but living always with the hollow, tormented feeling of knowing that one day I'd return, that one day, I'd have to return.

Odd to think that day should be the day of my only daughters wedding, but so be it, what is, is. I accept my fate completely'.

'Wow, that's pretty harsh' I considered out loud, 'not even invited to your own daughters' wedding? So…you're crashing it?'

'Perhaps… it would seem so' he said reflectively, 'on the other hand, I was the one that deserted her, not the other way around…Why would she even imagine bothering to include me' and as he spoke, he looked down sadly, dejected. I could tell, I watched his big frame seem to shrink down. Gosh, I began feeling sorry for the guy at that point, and I didn't even know him, or have any idea whether or not he was telling me the truth or making it up as he went along. I felt badly for him, even if he was a fruit loop, at the moment he appeared to be a very sad fruit loop. Maybe he was making it all up and believing his fabrications himself along with everything else he was telling me. Isn't that how psychotics work? Maybe though, he was telling me the absolute truth. How could I possibly know?

He could've been a very well dressed serial liar for all I knew, a socio-path. I had no way of knowing, or, of even guessing where he'd gotten all the props, the Italian licenses and all the foreign money. I was confused and simply didn't know what to think or to believe.

Felt that I just couldn't hurt him any more by being cruel or insensitive, by driving him away. What if he was telling me the truth? 'Well…what about love?' I asked, 'doesn't love have any part to play here…I mean…she is your daughter… isn't she?'

'Ah, yes, love, of course, love, indeed' he smiled good naturedly, 'love always has a part to play in everything. However, I'm of the mind that the deed has been conjured by my former wife, she'll be bitter about me until the very end.'

'Wow…your ex-wife' I told him, 'your life is like a television program. You've been married all this time?' I asked harmlessly, not expecting a reply.

'Ah, she, my friend, is the very reason for me exiling myself to my fates as such in Italy all these years. Stinging me mercilessly with missing the love of our beautiful, only daughter, punishing me to endure missing her going from being a girl into becoming a woman. She will never forgive me, not ever. That, is most likely the reason I wasn't invited.'

I was mesmerized, feeling like I was in a foreign movie. 'It's always the woman' I told him laconically, not meaning or intending to be funny, just generally speechless about what he was telling me.

'No friend' he rebuked, holding up his large hand to stop me from further conjecture, 'blaming her would be too easy, it's I that is to blame.'

'For what?' I questioned lamely, 'abandoning and exiling yourself to Italy for twenty-five years?'

'Precisely' he spoke tersely, nodding his head like it was attached to his body on a spring, and 'I could not stand the thought of not being loved by her, but especially by her, mother of our child. My heart was wounded beyond repair, I panicked and selfishly threw myself into complete and reckless abandon.'

'Oh, I thought we were talking about your daughter, not your ex-wife'.

'My meaning is of them both, she's not my ex-wife as you say; we never divorced, and as for my daughter, I'm not even certain she's my daughter at all, but the daughter of one of my old best friends from long ago. Someone I used to think of as an oldest, dearest friend. Several years they lived in discreet, mutual complicity of my deception, until at last, disbelief, lead to livid suspicions, until I could no longer endure living with suspicion at all. I confronted them…her, and she told me in his presence, quite unemotionally, she simply no longer loved me. That she hadn't for a long time, and that she wasn't responsible for how she felt; that it was just the way it was, she said.

'Get over it' she told me, and I remember her telling me she was sorry for that, but that's the way she felt, as if that; was going to make 'everything' better. I…I abandoned…my practice, my colleagues, not even knowing what I was doing or where I was going. I was fleeing, feeling like I was suffocating, blind with rage and humiliation, consumed by anger and betrayal.

I couldn't even think straight, I found myself in a taxi-cab gasping for breath and when asked where to, all I could say was the airport, the next thing I knew I was on a flight bound for Europe.'

'Wow' was all I could say. If this guy was a nut case, he told a great story.

'Therefore' he said brightly, 'as you see, today is the day I return once and for all, to attempt bridging the past with forgiveness, and to proceed emotionally unencumbered into my own personal future unknown, whatever it be.'

'You haven't seen your wife in twenty-five years? I asked incredulously?'

'Nor my daughter, who was almost two when I left. And how, I ask you, how do you ever live with regret? You don't I tell you; I've hungered insanely all these years just for their love. I can no longer live with regret; life is too short and too precious to spend it on 'anything' not done. Not done ever. There is only going on from here.'

'That sounds kind of optimistic' I told him buoyantly, 'so; you're just going to show up at your daughters wedding unannounced and uninvited?

'That is categorically my intention my friend. My wife, who has of course, remarried shall have the opportunity to see and to experience for herself, the love, that for all of these years, could have been hers and hers alone'.

'What about the guy who used to be your best friend, how's he going to react to all this? Does he consider her, his daughter?'

'That my friend, is a matter only made meaningless by the joy of our daughters wedding. Regret, I've come to believe these past twenty-five years can be undone by nothing short of forgiveness. Only by forgiveness is it possible to set free our minds from things we cannot change. After all, is it not so, that it is better to have loved and lost than to have never loved at all?'

'Something like that I guess, but wow; your former wife, former best friend, your daughter, wow…I wish I could be there.'

'Precisely my friend, it's bound to be a memorable experience for all, but remember, when you die, all you take with you are the best moments of… your life. This; I guarantee is going to be one of mine'.

I was as confused as I'd ever been in my life. I wasn't even sure any of this was really happening (again). No one, I knew, would believe me if I tried to explain Dr. Ekkertman. Knowing that truth is always stranger than fiction is something I'm very familiar with. I was having trouble believing all this, myself.

And like I've told you all along, if 'anything' could happen, it would and it did right at that moment. I watched Dr. Ekkertman's face suddenly noticeably brighten like a light had been switched on inside, behind his happy face. He straightened his posture from leaning on the counter to standing as tall as the awning would allow. I followed his gaze, and turned around to look behind me.

A young couple was approaching the counter. She was Japanese, slender, tall, quixotically beautiful, and the man accompanying her, a deeply ebony complexioned man with magnificent shiny cascading dreadlocks and a smile that could light up darkness. He was a photographer, she, apparently a journalist, both had laminated I.D.s on ribbons around their necks. They were beautiful together. They wanted coffee; Asian coffee was fine they said smiling. While serving their coffees, Dr. Ekkertmans' voice melodically filled the intimate atmosphere. I looked into the Japanese woman's face as she began giggling, covering her embarrassed face with her free hand, laughing. The dreadlocked man with her laughed as well; without knowing why. 'What did he say to you?' he asked her? In that moment, Dr. Ekkertman had spoken to her in fluent conversational Japanese as though it had been his native tongue. 'What did he say?' asked the handsome black man smiling.

'He wanted to know' she told him covering her mouth, 'if my parents knew we were sleeping together...' Even I could see the black man blushing. I turned to look at Dr. Ekkertman, 'I'm making the memories I'm planning on taking with me when I go' was all he said.

'I thought you were returning here with a mended broken heart, seems to me you're just about up for 'anything'.

'And hope I am until the end my friend' he replied, tapping the counter three distinct raps. 'Life is too good not to have good life experiences, and I want them all, right up until the moment I die' he said emphatically. 'Isn't that what happens normally, we live right up to the moment we die?'

'But is it living? Most people sleepwalk through the greatest experiences of living their lives, of simply being alive…of finding yourself wondrously alive; loving every single moment of being. Owning your own life. That, takes courage, forgiveness becomes a second nature'.

'You can say that again' I told him, 'a lot of things go on I can hardly believe myself', like that he'd just spoken fluent Japanese when I had him figured as a fruit loop.

'That may be true' he told me, 'however that's, the best part of living at all, when life's so real and true you can hardly believe it yourself… it's like magic happening'. I turned momentarily to resume work, considering what he'd said, realizing the truth of what he was saying.

I turned to face him and discovered to my complete astonishment he'd completely vanished as silently as he'd first appeared. Simply disappeared, gone, as if he'd never been there at all. I paused, curiously looking around for him. He was nowhere to be seen. This entire interaction with him had taken place all within about twenty minutes, and afterwards, what I had left of the encounter with him was what he reminded me of. That life is good. He encouraged me to wonder about just how good life can get. I thought about him for the rest of the day; couldn't get him off my mind, and realized no one would ever believe me if I tried to tell them about him. If I tried to tell them about what he'd said, and realized they'd have to find out about life and about love for themselves.

CHAPTER 9

'THERE COULD BE ANGELS'

As you may have assumed by now, I've never been, what you might think of as religious in any meaningful way, however; in attempting to live as a spiritual person, I must acknowledge that 'wonderful' things do seem to happen from time to time. Random, indescribable acts of happenstances that confirm my very own observations of wonder occurring. Believe it! Some things just cannot be explained. Is it timing? Luck? Coincidence? Chance?

There was the time, I thought of myself as working too hard to need being lucky on top of everything else. I was living the dream. I had my hands full just keeping things going, and believed, as I still do, that we create our own luck. Working that hard at anything often makes things appear easily done by anyone watching. So what seems impossible; is not always obvious. After my last encounter, I was open to about anything life brought my way. I was having an exciting time dealing with the unknown, dealing with the possibility of 'anything and everything' being possible. It made me feel really alive and I loved it. Man…I believed, I really did. I believed that if life truly was a dream, I wanted the best dream I could ever have, not some endless nightmare I couldn't wake up from.

Confidence in myself became the bulwark of doing my best, to be the best. It meant resisting fear, not thinking about it or focusing on it. Losing was not an option. Living without fear began being fun and having fun began making me feel even more alive. As if, 'anything' was possible, because I suspected that it was. I surrendered entirely to living without fear, without fear of failure, without fear of success, just without fear. It made me feel almost invulnerable; having accepted that there was actually very little I could do about the future anyway, except prepare for the possibility of 'anything'.

I began believing in random acts of wonder, believing that from moment to moment-in life, there is no way of knowing what's going to happen next. It's probably better that way.

I began believing that that's what the wonder is. Whatever comes might be terrible, but…it's possible…it might also be wonderful.

And so I began believing that future possibilities would be wonderful because they could be. And because I was working that hard at making them true, dedicating, with my entire heart and spirit in the right places, pounding it out sometimes, fourteen hours a day. Believing in wonder enabled me to have a great attitude about being successful. Believing in wonder made me suspect what Daniel must have gone through in the lion's den. Trust me; it wasn't all roses or Dim Sum; that's for sure, I've paid some serious dues to sing the 'I'm not Chinese Blues'. Anything in life comes too easy; beware. Nothing in life is easy and anything that comes free; probably isn't worth even having in the first place. The only thing in life that's free is advice and that's usually only worth whatever you believe it to be worth.

Actually, when you get right down to it, do you ever really know what's going to happen next? You just naturally do the best you can from moment to moment, and then, go on from there. Right? Well I was on a mission, that mission was living a purposeful life. I was the 'value added' to myself because of how completely I believed in what I was doing.

I saw myself as a wandering nutritional minstrel, a food apostle, a traveling noodle merchant dispensing the wisdom of nutrition through rice, veggies and boatloads of noodles. Everyone loves noodles. If it became necessary to become Chinese for a little while, I'd keep on pretending. I wasn't proud; I just did whatever I had to do until the show was over.

Several years deep into noodling history however, of doing shows all over, of sales volume constantly growing and the future looking brighter and brighter all the time, made me realize I needed help. Finding good help became more and more of an issue. Instinct told me that with the right help I could do more volume, be more successful, and that's when I learned the truth, that finding good help isn't easy. And if you do find good help, it's either because you're lucky or a miracle occurs because usually, you need them a lot more than they need you, no matter how much you offer to pay.

Sometimes only divine intervention can save the day, and that, doesn't happen very often. Besides, I didn't think I needed that kind of help anyway. The kind of help I needed, I needed now, right away, for a big show.

I hired a friend, a terrific, capable waitress from a local restaurant and made arrangements with her to meet at the show. I felt relieved; felt I'd been a prudent businessperson. Anticipated success. Knew you couldn't count what you hadn't gotten yet to count.

Felt I'd been ever so careful not to even begin counting my chickens before they hatched kind of thing, and being glad that I was at least that smart.

Trust me, never allow yourself to feel too safe; feeling too safe is generally the first sign revealing impending chaos. These events I'm telling you about, are like time-lapse calculations. The window of opportunity is open for very specific times, after that it's a ghost town. It's absolutely necessary for everything to be in place when the show begins, ready for the great bustling release. I was holding back the main spring of the machine, waiting to let it begin unwinding, ready to pounce forward. Really ready, only thing holding us back at that point; was beginning.

Friday afternoon the show opened. Everything was in place to let the machine begin unwinding. How could anything go wrong? Everything was lit, up to temperature, roaring to go, the only thing missing was help. The machine began slowly unwinding, then, unwinding faster and faster, I started panicking a little, where was my help? Going into the dinner hour, I began getting nervous, where was my help? I was becoming anxious, nervously concerned, but still holding it together. Suddenly, she appeared in the doorway POP! I sighed; gratefully relieved, knowing late in these cases is always better than not at all.

She looked so pretty; she tied on her apron like she meant business, I liked that, we were ready now for anything. I estimated sales could go up fifteen, maybe, even; twenty per-cent, because of her. I understood completely how necessary it is to hire qualified people.

She looked great in her apron, and acted just as natural as ice cream melting on a cone, she was perfectly congenial and her personality, as buoyant as cork. I sensed prosperity, and prepared full steam ahead, ready to go for broke. The machine began unwinding even faster during the dinner hour, the pandemonium became more than the two of us could manage. It was wild, I loved it, and it was exciting, like surfing on life and trying to stay on top of a gigantic wave.

It was like a huge surging wave going right over our heads. At the most crucial moment, with people three deep at the counter, she stopped, statue- like, in mid order, turned to looked at me with giant teary green eyes and blurted out that her husband was divorcing her and there was no way she could stay and help me because she couldn't even help herself. She took off her apron, handing it limply to me, beginning to cry even harder. I felt like I was on a game show. Everybody was standing there, waiting, eating, listening and watching. It was better than reality T.V.

With a heartrending look upon her face she simply walked out crying hysterically, telling me she was sorry, not seeming to realize the position she was leaving me in. I felt terrible for her, even worse for myself. Actually, the entire issue made me pretty angry because I'd prepared so diligently and was now 'on stage' in the thick of an opportunity window, which wasn't the time or place for processing anything else except Chinese food. Realizing the terrible position I was in, when no one was there, I turned and punched the wall in complete frustration, immediately breaking my thumb. Realizing instantly what an idiot I was. My hand swelled up like a discolored beach ball almost right away, quicker than before I realized things were definitely not going the way I'd imagined them going. The next day, having hardly slept because of pain, knew as soon as I opened the trailer, there was no way. I told myself there had to be a way, I stood to loose a considerable investment. But really, there was no way, my hand looked like an inflated purple cartoon hand and really hurt. I was driven solely by my motto; that the only way of eating an elephant is one bite at a time with lots of chewing between bites. I prepared, as always, for doing my best, but resigned myself to going down with the ship like it or not. I knew there was no way of saving myself; I was going down with the ship like an anchor, and becoming bitter about loosing after working so hard to be successful. My best efforts gave new meaning to buffoonish futility. Only accepting the possibility of impending doom enabled me to endure but; that, was about it. I wouldn't have hesitated a moment at that point to telephone the answer man if I'd known his number, but rejected the idea only because I knew, there is no answer man. I was the answer man, and even I knew that the answer was that the Chinese guy was 'toast'. I thought, only help from beyond for this foolish person could make things right, and that, was not very likely to happen. In my private thoughts I asked spirits greater than myself to pity this idiot.

What did it matter if I went down with the ship? Without help, I was still sunk. And moments like these are when strange things begin happening, just before the water washes over your head and you suspect all is lost.

Two nicely dressed women and a man wearing a suit and tie walked up to the counter. I over heard one of the women making arrangements with the guy in the suit to 'wait here' while they craft shopped. As him and I made eye contact, he told me that he hated craft shows. I raised my eyebrows. I watched his eyes take notice of my bulbous purple hand.

'That looks painful' he said, noticing me wince in using it. I raised my eyebrows again and jilted my head, 'only when I use it' I told him.

That's when it happened.

'Can I ask you a question?' said the guy in the suit. I looked at him with an expression of dubious surprise. 'Is it possible I could work in there, with you in your mobile kitchen while my wife and her friend shop around? I hate craft shows and I've always wondered what it was like to work in a food concession.' I stared at him in disbelief. 'You're kidding me right?' I replied, 'look, I'm not really in the mood for jokes…' 'No, no, I can see that' he told me. 'If I could…if you'd let me, I've always wanted to try my hand at this kind of thing. And it looks like you could really use some help with your hand the way it is'. This was just too good to be true, it could only happen to me I thought, but I remembered to remember the positive outcomes of anything that can happen. I took the bait, 'yeah I could use some help' I told him, 'c'mon in and put on an apron, do what I tell you to do, work safely, don't get hurt and I'll pay you when you're ready to leave'.

'Oh, you don't have to pay me' he said taking off his jacket and tying his apron on over his shirt and tie. 'This looks exciting' he said, 'just tell me what to do and we'll get to it O.K?'

He looked totally out of place. Like having Jeeves, the butler aproned up at the service counter, prepared for delivering up buffet at a royal gathering or something similar. He had on cuff links. He clasped his hands together again gleefully excited as the first customer of the day approached and gave her order. 'Oooh' he said handing the prepared order to the customer, 'doesn't that look good enough to eat?' he asked placing the order on the counter. He turned to look at me, childishly thrilled that the client had even left him a tip, 'she tipped me' he said excitedly. Even in agonizing pain I began feeling hopeful. Providence is a strange thing like that, you never know how it's going to occur, take shape or appear. He put his hands together again turning to me and said 'hey, this is really fun. What's next?' He caught me off guard,

'What's your name and what do you normally do?' I asked him. 'Oh...I work in a mortuary' he told me noticing the expression melting down over my face. 'No, oh God no, not in that capacity, entirely administrative stuff, you know, all paper work and billing, I never get to see anybody, this is fun! What's next?'

The machine began unwinding relentlessly with amazingly controlled chaos and by three o'clock that afternoon things were fast and furious. By best recollection we'd gone through two complete sleeves of platters or roughly five hundred orders. Going through that many platters is, in many ways of decathlon status, leaving you feeling like you've just run a marathon, and placed and haven't even yet caught your breath. We had just made some serious daily bread, and I couldn't have done it without his help. I don't think he was aware of that. I was prepared to be effusively rewarding and thankfully abundant to him. We were both weary with the fatigue of success when the sweetest little voice bubbled up unexpectedly, 'Honey...we're ready to go now if you are? Jason? Jason, you looked all tired out, what've you been doing since we've been gone? You ready to go now hon?'

I didn't even know his name was Jason.

'Well now' he said, 'that's the most fun I've had in a long time, but I've got to go now, is that all right with you?' he asked undoing his apron. Is that all right with me? This guy was killing me. He comes out of nowhere, works his tail off like a pro and then wants to know if he can go now, after helping me pound out a very profitable afternoon. 'No' I said, watching the look of surprise come over him. 'You've got to stay' I told him jokingly, 'finding help as good as you is hard to find'. The wife had a look of protest upon her face. 'It's time to go' he said, 'that was a ton of fun, but it was too much like hard work, but thanks' he said again handing me his apron. 'How much do I owe you?' I asked. 'Nothing' he said putting his suit coat back on and straightening his tie. 'How about a couple dozen egg rolls or something?' I asked him. 'No, really, I had a lot of fun, I hope that I've helped you out more than anything' he said stepping out of the trailer. 'Nothing?' I asked him one final time. 'Honest he said, 'but if you ever need me' he said handing me one of his business cards, 'just call'.

I took his card and looked at it. It was from a mortuary; presumably where he worked. I watched as he walked away with the two women, the card advertising the place where he worked had his name and under it was the motto: 'Help from beyond when you need it the most'.

I watched them walk away like it was the end of a movie. My hand still throbbed painfully. I couldn't believe what had taken place all afternoon; I was ecstatic. I never could've made it alone, I was certain of that. I realized the only way I could've made it at all, was with help from beyond, and it came at the time I needed it most. How strange is that? I came away with an understanding and a renewed acceptance that although bad things happen in life, the truth is, that good things also happen. But you've got to be open to it by accepting and believing they can happen at all.

It's too easy to become doubtful and cynical over time, just too easy to do nothing at all about anything but complain. The alternative is to imagine and believe in good things occurring. Call it angels or divine intervention, call it help from beyond I don't know, what I do know is that when it comes, very few deny it. The experience left me with a renewed commitment to myself, to live in a way that enables me to be a helpful benefit to everyone else; who just like me, are trying to do the best they can in living their lives. To joyfully 'pass it forward' because that's who I am and who I want to think of myself as being. It's an oddly pleasing feeling you get from living and being helpful, of giving of yourself, doing things you don't need to do, but do, because that's the kind of person you are. The ultimate experience of living a helpful, non-judgmental life is that it fosters in the minds of people you help, not something they may not remember, but something that they may never forget. And it leaves you feeling like a real hero.

CHAPTER 10

'WHEN THINGS GO WRONG'

"Impossible things are simply those which
so far, have never been done"

—Elbert Hubbard

E ven now, twenty-five years later, I'm still more curious than ever about how all that Chinese stuff went on for as long as it did. I tell myself it did because I needed the money. But do you ever have enough money? I suspect, not many people would ever confess to feeling they've got enough of anything. Still, what could've possibly gone wrong, especially when everything seemed to be going so right? How's it possible for everything that seemed to be going so wonderfully to become almost it's direct opposite?

Clearly this remains a yet unsolved part of my own life's puzzle and until I do, I suppose I'll never know how things could've continued to disintegrate after working and believing that hard, for that long. I was proud of myself for being that dedicated.

The problem had nothing to do with the fact that I was or wasn't Chinese. It was worse, and I knew it, but kept my feelings to myself. The show schedule I'd lined up was great and continually growing. We were doing Chinese at some of the best musical acts on the east coast, on and on from event to event we went, often selling out completely more often than not. That's what made me realize that though I was successful, I was also unprepared; that I hadn't planned enough.

I made it a personal business commitment never to say the words; "I'm sorry...we're sold out...' I told myself I'd rather put whatever didn't sell into a compost pile than say; 'I'm sorry I didn't plan far enough ahead...' I thought I knew my business enough to avoid pitfalls like not planning enough about having enough.

There it is, that word, enough. The truth seemed to be, that planning far enough ahead, and sometimes, even way beyond that, was the elemental key to success. Consider this, I knew my market, I knew my Keystone, I knew my Product, I knew my numbers and I was regularly hitting and going beyond my target numbers. Brooklyn would've been proud of me; he would've marked those numbers down in green in the center column of his journal. Usually we were hitting those target market projections because of recognizing who they were and what shows they generally could be expected to attend. I booked show and event schedules based on this specific target market observation. These people were my crowd. These were people with disposable income. These people wanted good food made for them, nothing that'd been sitting in some warm over tray for who knows how long. These people wanted me, I wanted them; what could be more perfect than that? And; with great music in the background. How many people have live musical backgrounds at their jobs? It might sound a lot cooler than it was, actually; it was more like a job hazard after a while, especially after twelve hours or more of continuously really loud music. But hey-I; was determined to be successful and was paying to play, so I was willing to play hard, and that meant long hours of being and doing Chinese. After a while, I didn't even hear the music at events anyway, it became less like music I was trying to listen to, and more just like noise at work.

During this profitable mercantile mayhem, I couldn't help recognizing the inherent weaknesses of the business. We had difficulties getting beyond certain production numbers, especially in very specific time frames. The answer surprised me. It wasn't the business that was the problem, it was me. I'd become the greatest restriction to the business growing because I simply was incapable of doing it quickly enough.

The business model was base upon everything being cooked to order, it's what made us famous, more or less, and we were always popularly crowded. However, there was only so fast everything could go. I steadfastly resisted the use of heating trays, and other quick warm-over food fixes, that just wasn't what we were trying to be about at all.

We were all about NOW, right in front of your eyes. Sizzling, steaming, wafting smells that looked so good it looked like something you just had to have, looking like a lot for the price, steaming hot, made fresh. People often asked if they could have two plates, like I didn't know they were planning on sharing. I tell you, there's not much better in life than being next in some cases, and this was one of them. I personally knew every order. Yellow, purple, red, bright green and orange; (squashes, onions, peppers, celery, broccoli and carrots!) on a mountain of noodles or rice, with or without General Tso's chicken or shrimp, with plenty of plum sauce, Hoisin or chili pepper-garlic. We were definitely outside of the box and since then, I've developed great respect for anyone who can and does devour a plate full of noodles with chopsticks.

We were totally about fast, fresh, colorful food, plentiful and delicious, made to order, however; the unfortunate practical thing about that is; every order takes time. And there never seemed to be enough time, we were always a bit behind, yet hardly anyone minded waiting or opted out for a burger or gooey pizza instead. What could be done I began wondering to increase volume?

I'd considered adding a third wok to the kitchen. At the time, I didn't necessarily think of that, as being particularly as insane as it sounds now. It added the possibilities of new numbers to our regular numbers, and I knew that something with that potential, would've driven poor old Brooklyn probably right out of his mind just trying to keep track of all those numbers in different colored inks.

Imagine cooking in three woks burning on high all at the same time? Success bears greatly, upon being prepared, after that; it's all about timing and occasionally, lots of luck. Or freak strikes of it.

I confess, that you haven't really mastered cooking until you surround yourself with curious, hungry clients all watching you and waiting for their order, cooked in one of three woks, while deep-frying with your left hand, and keeping all those balls in the air without dropping anything or burning anything worse than Chernobyl. Hemingway would have loved the 'grace under pressure' element of it, but I don't know that noodles were ever his thing.

Suddenly, in the middle of cooking an order, I found myself wondering how long I supposed I could do it; this Chinese thing. Thinking about that began making me wonder if, after twenty years, I'd end up like Angelo. Betty? Or worse; like Brooklyn? Talk about broken toys...? I didn't like thinking about things like that; but they were practical business facets I just had to respect. There was only so much volume we were capable of producing within a specific window of opportunity; no matter how flawlessly we worked as a team. Then, when least expected, it occurred like enlightenment. The answer became obvious to me like a high-speed mental feasibility assessment, with graphs and charts all outlining one dismal conclusion written pretty clearly on the wall like it or not. I had become my own problem. Once again...the Chinese dude was toast. Talk about death by a thousand cuts, I began feeling anemic.

At this rate I'd soon be out of wok. I began feeling caught up in playing a game I had no possibility of winning at, unless of course, I was willing to chew off my own leg to compete. I came to see at this point that I'd already been chewing away at it, trying to be a success. Three woks? And, a deep fryer? OK, maybe I was delusional; I needed the dough. Outside variable costs were continually rising and becoming prohibitive. How big, I wondered, would I have to become just to make it all worthwhile? What I wondered, was enough?

I began having re-occurring visions of having to chew off my leg to get out of a trap I had hoped I'd never find myself in. Success can be wonderful, on the other hand, it can also be that trap. It had brought me full circle back to the very beginning again. How weird is that? Working that hard, to eventually become my own undoing? I'd become my own business cycle. My business model had become untenable. I found myself having to resist ever- present feelings of abject ambivalence and compliancy.

Look, there's only so big any business can grow without changing, and I; was the weakest link in that chain. I felt great about that.

There's only so much air any balloon can hold before it either bursts or flubbers flatuantly away into flaccid meaningless expiation.

I'd achieved that point which all businesses eventually reach; of either growing bigger, staying the same, diversifying, or coming to an end of life cycle and then; having to have to go on, from there. Maybe, I considered, not even enjoying myself as much any longer. The old days; that at the time were so hard; now began seeming so good, and a lot simpler. And, a whole lot happier.

Getting bigger implied the obvious need of more of everything, help, supplies, travel, larger vehicles, access to specialty foods, things and logistics I hadn't even yet considered. It made me feel sick to my stomach. I'd come so far, shepherded my success, been so consciences, so diligent, so dedicated, only to feel as if I'd run, as hard as I could, into a wall. It seemed as if I was back to where I'd started from so long ago.

But there was something worse. I troubled myself greatly about whether or not I wanted to expand and grow or stay the same; and that's, when I began letting the problem begin solving itself.

There's nothing, in my opinion, inherently wrong with enjoying a profit as the result of working hard to make a dream come true, of making something happen, of being an employer, of accomplishing a goal. If it were easier I told myself, more people would be doing it. But nothing ever comes from nothing, never has and most likely never will. So what's anything worth?

Anyone willing to work that hard, becomes the added value of a business, perhaps; the driving force behind the business's success, of satisfying a market need, employing people and offering alternative services or unique products for sale. We were definitely unique. We were a hard act to follow or to compete with after sausage grinders, fried dough, French fries, cotton candy, fried onion rings, hamburgers, hot-dogs and gooey pizza. There seemed to have always been enough food vendors to compete with. We held our own. Some did better than others, and don't think the event promoters hadn't noticed who was popular and who was not. Were we making money working that hard? Sure. But enough money? Well, that's, a different question. Even the promoters of shows began wondering if they were making enough money, especially from the vendors. The prevailing attitude seemed to be that if anyone was making that much money off of them, then they should be paying more for the privilege of doing so. And this; is where things started getting really weird, because now, we're talking about how people go about defining what 'enough' really means, at least, to them. Enough of anything is different for everybody but especially so, when it comes to money, as in; enough money. Is enough ever enough?

Every year events began costing more money than the year before. Every year, there were new insurance liabilities, licenses, permits, certificates and training seminars, none of them renewable, but all of them necessary to buy and acquire simply to conduct business and every year costing more than the year before. It became like buying the same thing over and over just to do business. Just to have the legitimate right to conduct commerce. There were so many permits, certificates, licenses; awareness training vouchers and inspection receipts on the walls of the trailer there wasn't much room for any thing else. I considered just taping wads of money to the wall in their place. That's because everything had become all about, making money. But mostly; all about making enough money.

In the dictionary 'enough' implies better than just breaking even. Well… maybe, but, how much more better than just breaking even?

Enough? What's enough? When does enough ever become enough? Does enough mean satisfied? Like, have you had enough? Does enough mean fulfilled? Like, oh what a wonderful life? I began wondering about it, feeling myself reaching the point where I knew I'd had just about enough of everything, and I wasn't even certain what it was I felt I'd had enough of at all. I tried imagining what it was I'd had enough, or not enough of.

That's when I realized that enough is closest related to self-satisfaction, but mostly to avarice (greed), which is way unnecessarily beyond enough at all. But also, mainly because by then, even enough, is never enough.

After years of business and business deals, I'd had many unique opportunities for witnessing the devastating effect money can have on people. When it comes to money and money problems, it's either because you have way too much of it, or not enough of it, and if you feel you haven't gotten enough of it, first thing you do, is begin looking for ways, any ways, to get more of it. It's like a sickness. Makes people act like they're from 'Invasion of the Body Snatchers'. It changes people. And not always for the better. It means being possessed by something that's never satisfied. Promoters of shows, who in the early days were friendly, were now distant, aloof; I thought maybe it had been my breath. Suddenly, everybody's fee's tripled and as a result of that; everyone else felt, well, gee, maybe I haven't made enough either, and their fee's tripled as well.

Prices at whole-salers tripled overnight and reduced volumes by forty percent. Double whammy. Apparently they felt as if they hadn't made enough either. As an overall result, work became, well, more like work. And that; was no longer enough. Even I was grumbling because I couldn't seem to make enough to buy my products, pay my help and make everything else seem to be worthwhile.

Temporary business permits that used to be two or five dollars were now fifty or a hundred for one or two days. Seems they felt they hadn't made enough yet either. Then there was the increased fire department inspection fee increase to make sure I had a fire extinguisher. Then, the inspector who inspected whether or not you complied with all the other inspection fee's and regulations. Then the electrical inspectors and their fee's and of course the always vigilant state department of taxation and revenue insuring their pound of flesh. It quickly got to the point that I was paying out literally, thousands of dollars for events before I could say that I had even made a penny for myself at all, and I was doing all of the hard work. They began seeing vendors as their cash cow and determined to milk it for every penny they could. I began joking that it was easier to work for the Mafia; at least you only paid the 'vig' ('vigoresh') once.

In a lot of ways, it simply just stopped being fun any longer because it began becoming more and more about money. But primarily it'd become about 'enough' money; or, at least, enough to make everything seem, worthwhile. Isn't that what drives markets after all? People believing something's worth what it's worth? Everyone's belief and confidence that something's worth what its worth is, not necessarily what its speculated value is. Everyone seemed to be complaining though about enough or lack of enough, either they just didn't, or just couldn't, seem to make enough or sustain things until they could make enough.

So...when, I began asking myself, when, does enough ever become enough, and I kept coming up with the same old answer, which is never. The entire issue made me feel kind of sad, like I'd been aiming for something a lot nobler and now, my mission statement didn't mean anything at all because I couldn't seem to make 'enough' to make working that hard worthwhile. Or afford to pay people enough to help me to work that hard.

I'd never before thought about what 'enough' meant to me at all. Have I mentioned that I know enough about enough, that I loathe the feeling of being had? I mean, what's the point of playing hard at a game you can't win at every now and then? The time had come that

I was the only one who couldn't raise prices without pricing myself out of business. I began looking at my leg in an entirely different way, wondering where I'd begin biting and chewing if things ever got that necessary. I began becoming bitter about feelings of fleeting success at the expense of working that hard. It began becoming difficult while at shows where all of our senses were 'on' not to let my feelings interfere with business, but my heart was simply no longer into it and that hurt me in a very imprecise, hard to explain kind of way. I realize now that I had no exit strategy in place. I had no fall back positions or options of action. The only answer I could come up with to solve my dilemma was first to recognize I'd painted myself into a corner, brainstorm some new plans while the paint was drying then, try to learn from the experience and avoid it from then on.

It wasn't long after this that people began recognizing me and calling me 'that Chinese guy' in public places that made me know for sure, it was over. Some places wouldn't even allow me into their events because they knew the local fire department hot dogs or the snowmobile clubs fried dough would be passed by and they'd come to us. Up to then, I just hadn't known how things would come to an end, and that yented up a lot of already pent up frustration. I'd been in business for twenty-five years, had lots of adventures, made lots of new friends, had lots of excitement, made some money, had lots of fun, worked hard, sold tons of noodles and rice, been successful. But now it was over and I had to learn to accept that and learn to know when to say when, and to believe it, and I didn't want to. Some of the hardest things to accept in life are the things you just don't want to believe.

But in the end, you learn to accept the things you can't change, hope you've learned from the experience and go on from there. What else is there? I didn't know what else there was, but I began feeling on the road to perdition and recognized the need to do something, anything, to save myself without getting or being bitter for the way things were turning out. It certainly wasn't turning out the way I'd envisioned it. I began hoping a sign or symbol would reveal itself to me and that would enable me to know how to go on from there. But if you know anything at all about signs and symbols, you already know they don't always make themselves obvious, unless of course, you happen to be actively looking for them. And so, I just carried on through the season's tumultuous event schedule, keeping an eye open for something I couldn't explain, only hoped whatever it was, would find me and reveal itself. And as always, are you ever really ready for it when it does come?

CHAPTER 11

'THE ONLY THING THAT MATTERS'

"Truth lies at the end of a circle"

—Elbert Hubbard

Over the years I've thought a lot about how I felt about cooking like a mad man for all of those years, feeling like Kirk on the bridge of the Enterprise calling constantly for more eggrolls, chicken fingers, shrimp. There're a lot of good memories just like anything else I suppose, and I wouldn't have continued doing it if it hadn't been profitable, but it really was an awful lot of hard work. I've thought about the army of people I never would have known if I'd simply gone to work everyday. As hard as it was, it made me who I am today, not Chinese, but I had to go through the experience to find that out. I suppose that if it hadn't been fun, profitable or meaningful it wouldn't have gone on for as long as it had.

When I finally accepted that it'd come to its' natural conclusion, I began wondering who I was after all of that, after all those years of not being Chinese? I needed to find some answers in my own heart.

When the answers finally began revealing themselves as I recall, it had been raining, really hard, non-stop for two days and my final show of the season, of my career, was being conducted with a backdrop that could have been right out of an Old Testament movie by someone like Cecil B. De Mille. Highlighted by a relentless, driving rain that went on non-stop for three or four days and nobody dumb enough to go out in that kind of weather. Glenda and Sheila had abandon ship hours earlier for warmer, drier clothes and higher ground leaving me to face the wet and cold by myself. 'It's your business', Glenda reminded me trying to make herself feel less guilty about abandoning me, 'Think of all the money you'll be saving by not having to pay us' she said. I'd already thought about that, and had determined to make the best of another bad situation, staying open after all of the other vendors had closed and vanished. I took pride in the fact that I was a professional. But mostly because you never know when someone, anyone, might just happen by and be hungry as well, rain or shine. I really wanted to go home to be warm and dry, because there isn't much worse on a rainy day than wet socks. I had a sizable financial commitment to this little event and didn't want to end up with a boatload of food destined for my compost pile and nothing to show for all this time in the rain. Besides, I told myself, I needed the money. Need can be a big determining factor in a lot of instances, and this was one of them. I wiped the water from the counters again and told myself; I could do it, and put the rain out of mind. Momentarily, I glanced up, seeing a couple approaching in the driving rain under the big umbrellas they both carried, and sensed I'd made the right decision about staying open. When they got closer, under the awning of my stand, out of the rain, I saw they were two little old people huddled together, side by side like two little children sheltering.

They began shaking off cascades of water from their umbrellas and raincoats appearing innocent, yet dependent upon each other. I watched for a moment, thinking about growing old, before approaching them, trying to imagine what they could possibly want being out on such a day. Questioningly I looked at the little woman with raised eyebrows asking if there was anything I could help them with. 'Oh, no' she said apologetically,

'We don't want anything, we just needed to get out of the rain while I run to get father here some cotton candy from the fair...it's a tradition' she said nodding her head to reaffirm the truth of what she was saying. She put her delicate, shepparding, white hand on the little mans fragile arm, instructively informing him he was to remain here until she returned. He mutely complied shaking his head as she briskly popped up her umbrella and scurried off into the rain.

An eternity of moments later, it was just me; and him, with an abundant awkward silence between us, in the cold falling rain, but I could feel him staring at me. I suspected he felt obligated to buy something. 'So', I said to him in an exaggerated voice, 'is there anything I could get for you?'

'Why, yes' he replied haltingly, his thin reedy voice wavering in the wind, 'an eggroll to celebrate would be very nice, thank you'. 'Then, an eggroll it is' I told him, 'by the way, what are we celebrating?' 'Why, today's my ninetieth birthday' he said with restrained mirth, 'ninety years old today'. 'Oh yeah?' I replied, looking him over, determining he looked pretty good for someone ninety years old. 'Well happy Birthday then, I guess that deserves a celebratory eggroll on the house'. I served him his eggroll on a little paper tray, 'Ninety years old huh? I said reflectively, 'tell me, in your ninety years of life experience, does any meaningful moment or experience stand out more than anything else in your opinion?' I expected him to tell me about something way back when, when he first got married or something. But he didn't. I handed him a napkin, watching his delicate, age spotted hands break the eggroll into tiny bite sized pieces. I felt as if I were watching a hamster eating. 'Stand out?' he questioned mildly as if he were really culling his memory banks, 'oh yeah, certainly, but it was so long ago and things then were very different. More about the good ol' days I imagined. 'I was twenty years old at the time and it was Christmas time, it was a Christmas I'll never forget'. I listened to what he said trying to imagine what any twenty year old would be interested in at any time. 'Some serious partying then, is that what's it's all about then granddad?'

'Weren't much of a party' he said soberly, 'but it definitely was a time I'll never ever forget in my life. Not ever' he said. 'Was Christmas special that year?' I asked him. 'Special?' he questioned blankly, 'it was horrific'. I'd noticed he repeated every question I asked before answering like he was considering his answers carefully. 'Witnessed some real close friends shot to death and blown up like a bunch of rag dolls' he said solemnly without shock, but factually, without emotion. 'Christmas that year, was in one of the biggest, final battles of world war two, the Bulge. It was the worst Christmas I ever had. I'll take that memory with me to the grave'. And at that very moment in the chilling rain at the fair, an even stranger thing occurred. At the very beginning of his recollections of that time in his life, both he and I seemed to be somehow instantly transported back through time to the very time and place he spoke of. Maybe it was the words he used or how he described it. At first, it kind of frightened me, unnerved me, but somehow I found that he and I, this little old man, had left the rainy fair grounds and found ourselves in a snowy forest on an extremely cold, windy, starry night. Shadows were louder than noises and the wind blowing through the trees wailed like a haunted, threatening warning. As he spoke, we were standing side-by-side in the snow, but surprisingly not cold, strangely sequestered in almost like a bubble that allowed us to be there, and yet not be there. We were in a snowy, blizzardy forest and the air smelled sickeningly heavy of spent munitions and explosives but was otherwise as silent as a tomb. I was dumbfounded and confused by listening to the little man, he wasn't a little man any longer but a ragged, bloodied young G.I. gravely wounded and deathly concerned. 'Right there' he said pointing to his left, 'was the last place any of us ever saw Traub. Gone in a flash like he never existed, just vanished forever in a big boom. There were explosions and automatic weapons bursting everywhere, it was so insane, so maddeningly, deafeningly insane you didn't know what to do, guys calling out for their mothers, it was terrible. I was completely traumatized. I was next to a new guy right there' he said pointing, 'got his brains splattered all over me, thought at first it was me who'd been shot, never even realized I really had been shot and didn't even know it because I was so damn scared and didn't want to die. I was sure my life was over'.

'What'd you do?' I asked timidly. 'What'd I do?' he repeated my question again. 'I did whatever I thought I had to do, just to stay alive' he said, 'I wasn't even really thinking, just reacting. It was Christmas time and all anyone could think about was home, being with people they loved'.'So... what'd you do?' I asked him again. 'I made my peace with God, certain my life was over, and out of nowhere' he says gesticulating with his hands, 'comes this huge tank, the snow is so deep, and no one can move, and on it comes like some giant monster. It's coming right at me, I was certain they could see me, but I believed they didn't. I wanted to close my eyes and pretend it'd go away, so I crouched down in the snow and waited for it to get closer, probably to kill me, I was sure it was the end'.

'In those few seconds, I felt so poorly about what'd happened to Traub and that other fellow, I prepared to die myself and when that tank got closer, I sprang up in the snow and threw a hand grenade into it's tread, but, I ain't no hero, I was just terrified. I turned to run away and some fellows behind the tank I hadn't seen shot me up, left me for dead. Getting shot, that's what, saved my life. I fell down in the snow, laying there floating around in la-la land, bleeding to death, and everybody thought I was already dead.

I felt like I was out of my body and looking down at it, thinking what a pointless thing it was to die like that, for what? It made me angry. I was giving up my life? For what? They all just went rushing right on past me shooting and blowing things up, leaving me lying where I was, to die. I didn't feel any pain or fear or anything; thought I was on my way to heaven. That's when I realized the importance of forgiveness. More 'n that, I realized suddenly, the importance of living and forgiving. Ain't no right or no wrong worth losing your life about, life is, just what is.

'I'll never forget that night, or those fellows that never got home again. Or me, being the only one surviving, and felt I had an obligation to myself, and to them, to never forget'. He had tears in his eyes; big tears, and he stood there staring with unseeing eyes, with a blank countanance on his face, still clearly seeing it all as if it were only yesterday. I watched him gently daub his tears with a very clean, folded white handkerchief he took from his shirt pocket. Those few moments made him a very changed man.

As he spoke those words, we were suddenly, back in the rain, under the awning of my trailer. Rain was falling heavily. I realized we really hadn't been there in the rain at the fair, that we'd really been in the snowy chaos of so long ago. But we were back now, and I was watching him delicately eating his eggroll, cutting it into little bits and chewing it thoroughly with precise tiny bites. I sensed he was masterfully controlling himself. I didn't know what to say, I felt as if we'd just had a collective out of body experience and wasn't certain it hadn't really happened; but we were back in the present moment and it was still raining. He chewed his eggroll delicately, silently, and meditatively. I was speechlessly bewildered; almost sorry I'd ever asked him for his most incredible memory. He said it was a sacred memory he'd carry with him in his mind and heart for the remainder of his life and would cherish by reliving it at will, intentionally never forgetting. I asked him if he regretted it. 'Yes' he said reflectively, he did regret it. He admitted to doing things in his life based on what he believed was right and good, never wanting to live with regret about anything, in any form. He told me that up until that time he'd done everything he'd been told to do, had followed orders unquestioningly.

'Until the very end of my life I'll be a victim of my own mind; helpless to not relive things I now wish I had never let happen. Obligated now, to never let go, no matter how much I just want to forget. It'll never happen'.

Then, almost as if on cue, his wife suddenly re-appeared, huddled under her umbrella in the hard rain that fell. She asked him if he was ready to leave the fair and go home. They were out of cotton candy she told him; they weren't even open. He stood there politely wiping his fingers on his napkin. I saw him as the frail little old man he had become, and it was difficult envisioning him as ever being threatening, a violent man of war. He looked at me with the full strength of his pale green eyes through his rimless glasses. When our eyes met I couldn't help asking him 'what do you think it all means'? He regarded my question as he finished chewing his eggroll, 'what do I think it all means?' he repeated. He held me firmly with beseechingly clear green eyes, 'the only thing in life that matters' he said, 'ever…is love and forgiveness'.

Life's too short and there just ain't no place at all, for living with hate or bitterness…that's what life means: Look Inside For Everything' he said smiling. He looked away, carefully folding his napkin like he was planning on re-using it, popped up his umbrella and walked away with his wife, like two little children off on an excursion in the rain. I watched them walking away and began wondering what had really happened between him and me, but his meaning was perfectly clear and unambiguous. The only thing in life that's ever mattered, or ever will, is love and forgiveness. They're not only the most difficult emotions to master, they're the most freeing.

When strangers walk into your life speaking undeniable truths, capable of carrying you through your own life, as your own beliefs, it's simple confirmation that you're on the right path. I may never see that little man again **in** my life's time, but his message will be **in** my heart forever as a way of helping me to be who I am, or think I am, or ever hope to become. For me, that doesn't mean either being or not being Chinese, it simply means being who I am and being loved and respected for that, and then going on from there.

CHAPTER 12

'GOING FULL CIRCLE'

Listen, I'm the last person in the world, who'd ever go all Dorothy Gale from Kansas before she ever ended up in Oz, but lingering sentiments aside, her self-discovery seemed pretty much the same as mine. The greatest differences between us being, the last thing I ever needed in my life, before coming to my senses, was Munchkins, ruby slippers or becoming a potentially used up, drug addled, alcoholic has been, before trying to recover from ever being an is, or a, was, at all. The price of that kind success; like a winner take all approach, just seemed, not worth the terminal velocity required for getting there, before burning out completely. Being a mental and physical crispy critter is no kind of way for enjoying fame or notoriety. She (Dorothy) was luminary, a star that burned itself out shinning too brightly; the loss is all of ours. But Dorothy's truth; is my truth, and is as simple as Kansas itself, 'if you can't find your hearts desire close to home, it either doesn't exist, or your looking in the wrong place for it". Except, I'd paraphrase that down into something like, 'if you can't afford to live the lifestyle you're trying to accommodate, maybe you're trying to accommodate the wrong life style'. Things change, all the time. Thank God. Changing your mind is just one of those things that change'.

'Or its corollary, if your life style isn't making you feel you're where you want to be, maybe it's the way you're going about living it'. That's something only you can decide for yourself; and it doesn't take deep analysis or life style coaching or anything like that. Either you're happy and joyful, or you're not, and if you don't know yourself, it ususally means you're so full of shit, you're believing, and living, your own deceptions. So, if you're not satisfied with yourself and the life you're living, you might want to consider trying to figure out why. Which is a lot like saying if you find you've dug yourself into a hole, first thing you do, is quit digging, and start cutting yourself in some stairs. And as you're doing that, ask yourself, if not now, when? Keeping in mind that, 'true change, comes only from within' ('Neighbors' Belushi/Aykroyd 1981). You might even live longer, just because you'll being happier, and, the sooner you get to it, the longer you get to enjoy your life that way. Capeche? We're not just talking about pleasures, or touchy-feely kind of stuff; we're talking about happiness, real, lasting, long-term happiness. Talk about pleasures? What about the pleasure of looking out for each other's well being? Secretly, all the time I'd spent lying there on that hillside in Spain waiting for Glenda, thinking about the past; I was wishing she would've reminded me about the price of having too much fun discovering what the cost of trying to live my dreams was going be.

Or before drinking all that wine the night before at Festival and thinking about everything 'd been through up until then. Only after drinking too much did I begin realizing the need to change my approach. I felt like I'd tried to embalm myself from the outside while looking for answers on the inside, been dug up, left for dead, and just lying around waiting for crows to start pecking at me. Not very festive to think about at all, but now, just thinking about Festival hurt. It's unlikely even an entire handful of Ibuprophen tablets would've helped. 'Nobody forced you', Glenda cruelly reminded me, 'to keep drinking wine; I'm not... that hung over', she said. At the time, it just felt like the thing to do, you know? Like, when in Rome... only in this case, Spain, so I did, which proves, that even now, my judgment may probably not be anything to write home about. Ask Glenda about it, watch, she'll give you that face, the face with the look, I've been telling you about, and, on top of that, she'll be able to tell, right away, we've most likely been talking. That; 'look', the one that makes you feel sorry for having ever asked at all. A look, all married men know, or learn to quickly come to know, a look women pretend not knowing anything about, or, its especially crippling effect on men. You ask, 'what's wrong?' they turn their heads away, delicately huffing, nothing, which really means, everything. Everything? And the thought of having to deal with everything at that point reminded me of an ant contemplating getting across the Grand Canyon to the other side.

This, poor, brain damaged, hung-over ant just wanted to lie down and hope nothing crushed it while it was lying there passed out, which is what I did once we got into the taxi cab. Arriving at the airport isn't such a vivid memory for me, but getting there in the cab was though. It seemed we were bouncing around in the back for hours. The driver was blasting really loud Fiesta music on a cheesey little sound system, driving with one hand on the wheel, frenetically snapping the fingers of his other, and singing along totally out of key really loud in Spanish. And so completely self-absorbed in his reverie, that it left us feeling he wasn't even aware we were there, in the back of his cab. And besides not being much of a driver, wasn't what anyone'd think of as a good vocalist either, though he was pretty carried away with himself. Guys like him usually have handy fake microphones stashed close at hand they can begin singing into when they get overly carried away with themselves. He was wearing a striped tank top with lots of dark curly chest hairs bursting out like he'd been taxidermied, wearing several chunky gold chains around his neck that contrasted with the toasted, well done color of his skin making him look like a tanning booth causality. He looked like a character out of a Lina Wertmuller film (House of Seven Beauties, 1975). But nothing could've prepared me for going through customs, brain damaged. Even beyond drawing unreasonable suspicion upon myself by shading my eyes from any brightness, like I'd been underground for the last fourteen years, it was Orwellian. All I could think of was 'Alphaville' (1965 / Jean Luc Godard). Beseechingly insisting to all authority figures, the need for keeping my sunglasses on, making myself suspicious, and all that. Thinking only of getting on the plane, into my seat, and going unconscious for around ten hours. If I was glad about anything, it was that Glenda wasn't as similarly brain damaged with a similarly debilitated frame of mind; we both could've easily ended up landing, somewhere in South America, lost, wondering how we got there in the first place. I realized how much I depend on her when we travel, especially when my body was in the fun repair shop, having work done, repairing my brain. She's capable of forgiving me but the cost of repairing my self-inflicted fun damage, is enduring her look that says, nothing, yet means everything. What seemed like it took all day to achieve eventually resulted in finally arriving at the airport. The driver tore the radial tires of the cab to pieces along the curb pulling in; the sound reminding me of my pancreas being ripped out. Still driving poorly with one hand, making it sound like the tires were being shredded, reduced to tormented strips of rubber around metal rims. Opening my eyes, I just assumed we had arrived at an airport where we exited the taxi; it was actually quieter outside the cab, even with jets landing and taking off. What grotesque pantomimes awaited us; all acted out in the name of security hadn't yet even crossed my mind. We necessarily began passing through multiple levels of security, each, acting out their part in their little security drama's for making us feel we were safe, by violently rifling through our luggage with rubber gloved hands and glaring at us as if we were suspected of criminal activity simply for traveling. 'Oh yeah?' and then the suspicious insinuations, 'where'd you get the extra cash to go on vacation…?' You know? That kind of hairy eyeball jazz, treating people overly polite, running their grimey paws wearing white latex rubber gloves over everything, latexically insinuating the muscle of their authority, acting the tiger, 'Senior,' waiting to pounce. I stood there, looking at my reflection in his sunglasses and saw myself looking pretty rough around the edges, unaware I was glaring at him, psychically refuting his narrowminded ideas that vacationing had something to do with why Ossama'd been so hard to find. I realized I would've probably stopped someone who looked the way I did too. Apparently, he hadn't guessed that it was because after Ossama had played his part, he'd been forgotten. At least, until Ossama needed apprehending, which was right before needing to be 'buried' at sea so no one could ever find him. Now, you know what everybody says about fish stories being fishy, nobody even knows where he is, or might be, aside from maybe being seafood. When was the last time you heard that kind of crazy stuff happening? Was that, supposed to make everyone feel safer? 'Oh? That guy? Yeah, well, a, we fed him to a lion…in the zoo…'

Finally, after agreeing to allow him to search me for weapons, we began taking our seats on the plane, after they had confiscated my toothpaste, shampoo and plastic razor. Man, I began feeling a lot safer. I was thinking more of some kind of sanctuary, but my mind was thinking more like some kind of botched escape attempt, like I was voluntarily breaking myself back into the prison I'd just successfully managed breaking out of. I began wondering if going home was anything I wanted to do at all. I was thinking about Dorothy, remembering all the things she loved about the farm back in Kansas.

Our massive Europa airbus throttled up, spun around like a toy before lurching forward in a growing, charging crescendo of power hurtling along the black ribbon tarmac prior to capturing flight. Its' landing apparatus violently shaking the entire planes structure, hitting every bump, crack and irregularity in the miles long runway. Now, I love flying, but this part, of every flight I've ever made, is always the sketchiest part of doing something I love doing. So, when it's happening, I keep reminding myself to believe, and keep faith, that the pilot's got mine, and everyone else on board's well being in mind as he goes about his piloting thing. I tell myself, there are times when you've just got to trust people because you're, not the one in control. I really believe that, I found it comforting to believe he knew what he was doing. Or, at least hoping he knew what he was doing.

The point is, while all this takeoff stuff this was going on, anything could've happen, gone wrong, or, result in one of the finest of human sensations, lifting off and flying like a bird. The seat belt sign was still on, I felt myself cinched into my seat almost too tightly, I began violently shaking along with everything else on board, realizing through those agonizing moments, my well being, being entirely out of my control. Wellbeing at that point, actually being out of anyone on boards control, and isn't that the way it usually is? Come on, when your number comes up, it's up, no matter where you are or what you're doing. Hope you enjoyed the flight. My number came up once, many years ago, changing my life forever, and was the only lottery I ever won, the draft lottery back in the sixties. Big win huh? But it did change my life, and believe it or not, in the long run, changed me for the better. It was what forced me into making some of my first important life decisions concerning my life and wellbeing all based upon what I believed. But, these anxious, pre-flight moments of doubt before take off precede the disbelief of the euphoric miracle of lifting off at all. Lifting everything, including me, up into the sky, as free as a bird, in something larger than a building. Faith is a wonderful thing; faith, as in; you believing that thing's really going to get off the ground and fly? I absolutely...do. I hope.

Of course, lots of people disagree that flight requires faith to believe in successfully launching gigantic super structures like modern jets into flight, as if they were paper planes catching an updraft. They rely on facts that say planes can fly, and do, and so, believe that because they can, therefore will, and that's all there really is to say about it. But this point of view requires the suspension of disbelief; that it can fly, or that it won't crash, because that; can't happen to me. That it might crash, or, that anything's possible, like a flock of birds might fly into one of the engines. Failure to suspend their disbelief leaves them believing for example that they believed they'd likely crash and burn, or worse, burn and then crash. I'm not saying that flight can't be done, or, isn't possible, only just that any number of random things could occur to alter its outcome, just like living the days of your life. So, once you get beyond the odds of getting that giant airplane up into the sky, the only other real concern, probably, is landing it. On the other hand, another consideration is, there are probably very few people who'd ever get on a jet they believed was going to crash. That, suspending that much disbelief, was just plain stupid. I know what you're thinking. So, there's no Santa Clause, no tooth fairy, or rodent that puts money under children's pillows when they loose a tooth? No…I could never be that cruel. What's gained by ruining anybody's dreams and wonderment prematurely? And so, as self deceptively cruel as it can be; there we go; pretending that things in life that aren't, really are, and things that are, really aren't, a novel commentary on our humanness; a concept that seems to work both ways oddly enough. Take climate change for example. An enormous number of people suspend their disbelief, believing that something that really is happening; really isn't. So go about living their lives untroubled and unconcerned, believing that because they believe it isn't really so, it isn't, so, why bother worrying about it at all? We could say; they're only fooling themselves, but why disappoint their expectations? Right? Ignorance is said to be bliss, isn't it?

So, this jet's blasting off, climbing and angling up, into everyone on board's future, and they're all believing at any moment, the delight of flight begins. Everybody's anxious disbelief that it wasn't going to, or hadn't; come abruptly to an end, everyone on board all believing that it would fly, because it was supposed to. I'm not certain that's too profound, but it certainly seems to be a statement about the power of having faith. Besides, having faith makes you feel good, and when you feel good, you are good, and that makes just living, seem indescribably incredible. I'm a firm believer in indescribably incredible. I live to experience as many moments of indescribable incredibleness as I can before I vanish into the future.

It makes me aware of the awesome random wonder and mystery of being a part of the Milky Way galaxy system. Does that; make me a star-child? Anyway, I'm strapped into my seat imagining the odds of anything going wrong, like the plane falling apart from all the shaking, before even getting into the sky. That; made me feel foolish, realizing even if the odds of something happening were, say, one thousand to one, this could turn out to be that one time. And then no odds at all would turn out to be the only better gamble. It only had to happen once. Have you ever seen a falling star? What are those odds? Have you ever made a wish upon one? After all, what's more sacred than that?

Suddenly, lift off, and a feeling of temporary weightlessness, free as a bird. My inner self, feeling faith has been edified. It didn't require any suspension of disbelief at all because anything that could've happened; fortunately didn't. In moments we're miles above the clouds, making me feel as if we've just gone over the rainbow where blue birds fly and everything's possible, it's why I love flying so much. Looking out the window, I peacefully realize, life's not defined in the final moments of living; or, by the hyphen between birth and death dates on your tombstone; it's defined by experiencing every single second of the world around you. Everyone who's ever lived, has had expectations, hopes and dreams, and discovered it's not always easy getting things done. Instead of worrying about things not done, thoughts and dreams come alive considering things, not done, yet. Then, reminding myself to worry about something else, begin seeking mindless distraction, like, watching a movie. Activating the video mounted in the rear of the seat ahead of me; reveals an almost invisible crack across the screen, not to be seen, unless it's on.

It becomes immediately obvious, watching any in flight movie will be virtually impossible, the crack causing the on screen images to be digitally disjointed, segmented unrealistically, comically, slightly offset. Adding to this, the head set for listening, is scratchy and intermittent, resulting in leaving chunks of movie dialogue missing. Together, problems of sound and screen are too painful for my brain in its present condition; eliminating the headphones I opt for making up my own dialogue for the digitally challenged movie on the screen.

So, sitting there, all buckled in, my mind becomes like an untied dory and begins drifting. Free and floating down stream, part of any current that carries it, creating the ambiguous headspace coming from watching a movie on that cracked screen. Staring at it, I see the cracked screen as a metaphor for life itself; requiring constant adjustments in thinking to compensate for distorted perceptions. This, is, I'd like to make clear, about a good life being the result of endlessly compensating for bad perceptions. And, if you're willing to make those adjustments in understanding an integral part of your life, it's done because that's who and how you are, without it being the result of any devious gain to be had by taking advantage of any crack. I felt kind of self- enlightened, like a new awareness occurring to me. I felt like Billy Pilgrim in Kurt Vonnegut's diabolically dark satire about the life of a man, (Slaughter House 5, 1980), helpless against arbitrarily floating backward and forward in time, experiencing the results of his own life choices. I was probably the only one on the plane with defective equipment; no one else seemed to be complaining, what were the odds? So, I sat there, seeing the re-occurring dream of my life, (which turns out to be a comedy by the way) playing out on the disjointed screen before my very eyes. I sat there watching, transfixed by the bear hug of considering the consequences of my life choices. Considering how I'd used my gift of life, at least, up until now, when I was aware of being more not Chinese than I had ever been. The re-occurring dream story I tell myself about living, whose intent has always been moving me up to a higher plane of consciousness and understanding, not just cluttering up my thinking with stuff I didn't want or intend to use. I sat there staring at that broken screen, remembering that little car crashing through my nirvana dreams back by the stream. About our mountain picnic celebrating our new beginnings, the orange juice, champagne and aspirins. The wild guitar music, the dancing and wine and tapas, the excitement of feeling that I was breaking into everything that's new and alive and good. And realized more than anything, I wanted to start shouting out loud over and over again on the crowded plane, like I was having a mental breakdown, 'I love my life! I love my life!'

But this; is where it gets even weirder. Every time my mind begins playing or re-playing the movie of my life, my actual self seems to perform some kind of editorial oversight, updating large segments of dialogue and event, as strange and wonderful as they are, as if it were being explained by subtitles in a foreign language. And I'm OK with that, because aside from other considerations, my life is not boring, but a lot more challenging than you might think, like a comedy-documentary, if there is such a thing. For example, imagine a clown doing in depth analysis and commentary on Freudian theories of 'self'. And that, reveals that lifes pageantry and enjoyments aren't always based on understanding how things work together or alone, and; is something not shared equally by everyone. This might be because everyone's got movies of their own, going on all at the same time, (even if they're unaware of it). And that; is a movie unto itself, sadly, not always a very happy one. I took the screen for as long as I could before switching it off, and devoted my attention to my voracious shark like feeding frenzy appetite for reading, and reread 'Great Expectations' by Dickens on the flight. My abounding empathy for it, causing me to consider it being more appropriately re-titled 'Extraordinary Disappointments'. Which demonstrates quite clearly, how pointless it is in paying more attention to other peoples lives and dreams, and not enough to your own. I mean, the future is yours, and is always at hand, always there, at the very tip of your nose with you staring straight into it, most often without you even being aware of it. What's it going to be? Feeling confidently inspired by the effects of living long enough just to get older, maybe even a bit wiser? This whole experience of being either Chinese or of not being Chinese, right up to drinking too much wine at Fiesta enabled me to learn to look forward to life's challenges. Taking an active role in being part of the swirling, spinning, whirling vortex of what we call time, finding happiness with the choices I make in dealing with all the unknowns. Call it synchronicity, or call it poetic timeliness, but at that exact moment, in the midst of my deepest introspection, Glenda, whom I thought was sound asleep, reaches over and touches my hand, at once connecting me with the entire universe. And, in that moment; suddenly realize, this, is it. This; is how it comes to an end. And when it does, I find myself loving who I am and the life choices I'm making, and doing what I love to do, and loving every moment I'm spending my life by loving myself. BAM! I'm a lucky guy because I've finally gotten my head out of my ass! I've finally come to know it's not always easy being who you are or may hope to appear being, (or, in some cases being who you aren't), but is always necessary for loving who you are. And if it helps, reminding yourself that of all the changes you can make in your life, the most important is remembering you can always change your mind, and your thinking. And also, of the wisdom of Shalom Alikum who reminds us that in all laughter, there is sorrow, and in all sorrow there is laughter, because in the end, laughter and crying is all that saves us from just being ourselves.

CHAPTER 13

'KITCHEN TAO—WAY OF THE WOK'

I've spent the last thirty years working in an easily hazardous environment, a commercial kitchen. Our success was based upon our ability to produce enormous quanties of food as quickly as possible, insuring to reproduce each order looking and tasting the same. I am happy to say that in all those years, through all those crazy events, dealing regularly with hundreds and hundreds of pounds of noodles and rice, and everything else, no one ever got hurt in any way, particularly, me. Over time, experience taught me the necessity of learning respectfulness to your place of labor, particularly ones with dangerous scalding oil, open flames, sharp instruments, and tons of distractions, which are always potentially hazardous. So whether your kitchen is a high paced production facility, or your own personal kitchen at home, a cultivated respect for everything that goes on in a kitchen is fundamental to becoming a 'good' chef. I assure you, there is never any need for aspiring to perform like the Ginzu Chefs speed chopping, dicing, slicing or making Jullian Fries on late night food channels to be considered a 'good cook'. Learning to become confident and comfortable working with sharp tools, boiling oil, and open flame is part of learning the craft of operating a kitchen safely and, wearing the many hats doing all that, requires, and 'speed' chopping, dicing, slicing and whipping out tons of Jullian Fries, is meaningless. You want to prove something? Prove it to yourself and be careful in the process.

Simple beginnings are the best for beginners, you'll need a cutting board that accomodates you, I prefer wooden surfaces, but acrylic is also good. Then, honor your labors and make it easy on yourself by acquiring a set of hight carbon content cutting utensils, and this is important because when the metal surface of your utensil contacts your ingredients, low quality, low carbon cutting tools can and will stain the food making it look unsavory. I have always operated using what I know to be a 'Cricket', an eight-inch long, by two-inch wide high carbon content cleaver type of utensil. You may find its wide blade, and handle easy to grasp, and manipulate in an array of prepatory styles. One of the advantages of this type of cutting utensil is that by laying the unsharpened backside of the cutting edge gently against the fingers holding the food being prepped, you always know where your fingers arent. Be careful, have fun and be adventurous but be present in mind to what you're doing. Having proper, quality equipment makes cooking easier and more enjoyable, so in addition to a safe working commitment to yourself; these, are the beginnings of good kitchen tao.

What you're doing in your kitchen; is creating the love you give to others by feeding them delicious, well-prepared food that speaks volumes of that love. On the other hand, that's one of best reasons why there's always doors on kitchens in restraunts, they don't want you to see what's going on back there, and in a lot of ways customers are probably better off for that. But the secrets to success in cooking Chinese food don't have to be hidden behind doors, and that's no secret. But if there is any secret at all to successful Asian cooking, it's the understanding that all success lies in good preparation. The reason for advance preparation is because when cooking finally begins, it occurs rapidly, often at the hightest, hottest possible temperatures for rapid searing and braising, therefore, preparation beforehand is essential. Attempting to prepare ingredients as cooking gets under way is the quickest, and, most disasterous path to an unfulfilling cooking experience, as well as the quickest way for experiencing what I call 'the Cherynoble' effect of burnt food. Adequate advance ingredient preparations make cooking easy, because each step in preparing all reciepes require time to achieve, before yeilding eye appealing color, flavorfully tasting, delightfully textured and rich, irresistably fragrant boqouets and savory sauces. Consider the culinary wisdom of an hour to prepare, an hour to enjoy, and several hours to reflect upon the delightful experience.

After necessary preparations, your culinary confabulations will be created and ladeled from a blessed vessel, your wok, being served up as finished dishes. A quality wok is the unique cooking vessel used for heating and cooking your assorted reciepe ingredients into becoming savory tasting sensations that announce their presence by their abundantly distinct cooking fragrances. Cooking in a wok is fun; and every stir-frying event becomes an adventure unto itself in becoming a better cook. When people used to ask me how I learned to cook Chinese food, I told them, honestly, I was still learning. And I was, with every order I cooked. And, the better I got and the more knowledgable I became about how to go about it, time after time, the more I enjoyed doing what I was doing. The truth is, whenever you do anything for ten thousand hours, you either get really good at doing it, or have a mental breakdown. The better you get at anything, the more you'll do it, the more you do it, the better you'll get. Sounds crazy how something like that works out huh? Sounds like a childrens song about doing things over and over, again, but somethings, really do need doing over and over again. And one of those things associated with becoming a better cook is learning the need to 'season' your wok over and over again everytimer you use it and to keep it seasoned before and after all use. Cleaning your wok is not the same as seasoning it. Rinsing your wok with water after use is typical, seasoning it is burnishing the natural food oil residue to coat the steel, primarily to keep it from rusting. Refraining from using detergents when cleaning your wok is recommended as detergents tend to breakdown the seasoned layers of natural food oils tempered into the metal itself by cooking. Removing these layers of cooked in food oils leave the metal open to rust which leads to loss of metal temper, especially at high temperature heat.

Losing this tempering will immediately show when you begin cooking as uneven burn spots in the heated metal wok everytime you begin stirfrying, which in turn, will burn your food. This can only be avoided by cooking in a carefully seasoned wok and is why seasoning your wok, and keeping it seasoned, is so important. Seasoning your wok is accomplished by simply heating it up to high temperatures, then ideally, oiling with a few drops of Sesame oil as it begins cooling and rubbing the oil into the cooling metal pan as you wipe it clean, preparing it for storage before you cook with it again. This seasoning allows your woks to age into a cooking companion you will come to know and trust for what you can produce cooking in it. The more you come to cook in your wok, the more you will realize that growing successful as a cook is not only accomplished by knowing your ingredients, but also by knowing the equipment you depend upon for successful cooking. People you are cooking for will come to love you for this knowledges and everything it enables you to create.

The creation of food looking good enough to eat is your goal because the truest observation about hungry people everywhere, is before ever tasting food, feast with their eyes first. Now everyone obviously has their standards, but generally it's a case of something looking so right, it must be good enough to eat; as so, it gets either eaten, or it doesn't, it's as simple as that. And forget about how something might even taste, if that something doesn't look good enough to eat, it's generally assumed that it probably won't, or doesn't taste that good either. As simple as it seems, this is actually how food really makes people think. Well…how do you tell? Well…just look at it. This is perhaps the most elemental lesson to learning about cooking, presentation. Making every dish look not only alike, but good enough to eat is one thing, but serving it and presenting it are the ultimate goal. Learning to become a confident, capable cook is much more than just simply learning to cook food and more about how food is simply cooked, time after time after time. Seeing in some cases; is really about believing and this is one of them. People standing at the counters waiting to order always took notice of someone else' order, examining it, deliberating to themselves before saying, 'oh, that looks good, I'll have too'. I didn't have to sell them anything; the product sold itself. I just had to get comfortable with making the same thing over and over again hundreds of times.

Compositions of simple, harmonious foods of varying color, in thre hands of a master can yeild a palate of irresistibly delectable, succulently beauty morsels you can eat. Clients purchased our menu products with their eyes before ever tasting them or reading them from the menu board, and after tasting, rarely failed to devour it entirely. They confirmed their own beliefs, by eating it all.

In the concession world, a lot can be foretold about food by what's most commonly found discarded, partially eaten in the trash bins. Gooey pizza, greasy rancid sausage grinders buried in canned, grilled peppers and onions, fried dough with excessively oily leftovers, tempura vegetables coated with what appeared like a plaster based batter. I won't say ever, but, our food was rarely ever found in refuse containers, and if and when it was, it was usually because we'd simply served up too large an order. People came back thanking us, something not many do at fried dough rigs, French fry stands or hot dog-burger joints. Only time could teach how best to present the lowly vegetable, a thing my own mother should've learned, for she could've been guilty of crimes against food. Yet blanched, flashed, al dente, or succulently raw, they are what they are; beautiful foods rich in flavor and goodness, impossible to enhance by over cooking, over boiling, excessive steaming, grilling, smoking, baking or broiling.

The fact that each order was cooked as ordered, added an additional element of theater that everyone seemed to enjoy, especially when they, knew that they were 'next'. The sizzling aroma of garlic and ginger frenzied with rice wine vinegar and sesame oil brought people drifting in, claiming they could smell 'that' in the parking lot, and by following their noses, determined they had to have it. What I never let on about to them was that that; hadn't just happened by accident. It was better than any sign could've ever advertised. And…it was everywhere all at the same time no matter where we were. So, you might wonder, how is it done? The simple answer is the same way everything else is done, by knowing what you're doing and what you're doing it with. Learning the characteristics of your ingredients and what they're capable of singularly as well as in harmony with other ingredients will reveal flavors conceived first in your imagination, tasted on your imaginative tongue before ever actually being made. Learning by trial and error takes a bit longer, true, yet, sometimes, makes even better, more intuitive cooks. Cooks who can taste color, who taste with their minds, who can substitute ingredients with astonishing clairvoyance, leaving people smacking their lips, asking continually for more. You…want…more? Of course they do if it's good, of course they do. At this point I'd like to remind you, and warn you about being careful. Kitchens are terrible places to have accidents, you could for example, unintentionally knock yourself unconscious. Especially, if you're planning to put chili peppers in oil, at melt down temperatures. Never attempt to breathe in the smoke. These are implied temperatures ranging typically for a majority of stir-fry dishes as 360-to-385 degrees or almost 'smoking hot'; you'll clearly smell the roasting aroma of sesame oil. At that point, you'll either want to begin cooking assiduously or risk creating your own failure. But look, success at anything doesn't just happen, it happens because of all the behind the scenes preparation that make it possible, and only that, and lots of hard work leads to making it happen. The secret of success is to make it possible by keeping things simple. If you can, you can make a living doing it. As much as I've complained over the years, making good food for people has been a big part of my life. It's about who I think I am. Cooking, preparing and eating are things that connect us all in a necessarily needful, sustainable way. This is something I mean from my heart. Everything about eating well; is about realizing pleasures through the senses. Food that's produced by patient loving attention to detail and an almost fanatical attention to processes cannot fail to be good.

MOVIES TO GROW BY

'ALPHAVILLE' (JEAN LUC GODDARD 1965)

'GET TO KNOW YOUR RABBIT' (Aston/Smothers/Wells 1972)

'NEIGHBORS' (AYKROYD/BELUSHI 1981)

'THE LOVED ONE' (WINTERS/SOUTHERN/GUILGUD 1965)

'FEMALE TROUBLE' (JOHN WATERS/1974)

'ATOMIC CAFÉ' (I982)

'SLAUGHTER HOUSE FIVE' (VONNEGUT/ 1972)

'HOUSE OF SEVEN BEAUTIES' (LINA WERTMUELLER 1974)

'DESPERATE LIVING' (JOHN WATERS 1977)

'LO AND BEHOLD' (WERNER HERTZOG)

Obry Alan

Dec 2, 2018

CPSIA information can be obtained
at www.ICGtesting.com
Printed in the USA
LVHW040833111020
668494LV00003B/869

9 781951 343330